A Mouth Like His

"The mouth of the righteous is a fountain of life."
Proverbs 10:11

Faye Hake

Rivendell Press
Charles Town, WV

A Mouth Like His

Preface

This book is part one of a three part series conceived and born out of a few sentences from Colossians chapter three. There Paul describes to the Colossians how those who have received Christ Jesus as Lord and been raised with him have, *"Taken off your old self with its practices and have put on the new self, which is being renewed in knowledge in the image of its Creator."* (Colossians 3: 9-10)

These three studies aim to renew our knowledge of our Creator, so that we, through Christ, in our new self, may truly be like Him. We had forgotten our Maker but now we are reconciled to Him. "Being renewed in knowledge in the image of our creator" means recollecting His character. We do this by searching the Scriptures and by observing Christ," the image of the invisible God." Then we put on new practices that reflect the character of our Maker that we were meant to emulate in our tiny creaturely way.

These three studies, A Mouth Like His, Hands Like His, and Eyes Like His take an in-depth look at God's mouth, hands, and eyes. What were they like? What are they like? How might we reflect His image by having a mouth like His, hands like His, and eyes like His?

This first book, A Mouth Like His, is the most substantial of the three studies because the Bible tells us so much about both God's mouth and about the great potential for good or evil that our mouths have. In fact Paul, in these verses from Colossians three, brought all this up about "being renewed in knowledge in the image of our creator" in the context of pointing out how inappropriate slander, filthy language, and lies were in the mouths of those being re-made in the image of their creator.

In the language of the letter to the Colossians these three books are all about demonstrating the truth of "Christ in us, the hope of glory." They're about us learning to "live in Him, rooted and built up in Him" because "He has rescued us from the dominion of darkness and brought us into the kingdom of the Son He loves"- a kingdom in which we are free to be all He ever meant us to be when He made us in His image.

This series is written to an age integrated audience (roughly nine or ten years old right on up through adults) It is my hope that writing at a level that children can benefit from will not put off any of us teens or adults who so desperately need this hope-giving gospel-centered teaching. Adults, teens, and children have found these studies profitable. Dive into these on your own, or study together with the children in your life. The origin of these studies was preparation for our own family worship times and the discipling of our children. The applicability of the content across all ages provides excellent family worship material; but be prepared to learn more yourself than your children or your students do. Grown-ups have lived long enough to know how badly we need the grace of God to wash over the way we speak.

Table of Contents

Introduction

Stick out your tongue and say, "Aaaaahhh."

This is a course in which we will let God examine our mouths.

Our mouths are the most significant part of our bodies when it comes to potential for doing good or evil. Proverbs 18:21 declares, "Death and life are in the power of the tongue."

James informs us that if we could only control our tongue, the rest of our body would be kept in check. Unfortunately James doesn't appear to hold out much hope for us succeeding in that daunting mission. He says our tongues are "a world of evil among the parts of the body" and he tells us "No man can tame the tongue." That's about as bleak as it gets, God Almighty telling us to "give it up."

However, there's one loop hole we can cling to. And we will. "**No man**" can tame the tongue. Maybe this isn't about man (us) taming our tongues, maybe there's hope from another source. In fact there must be hope out there or God wouldn't have told us in another place (Proverbs 10:11) that, "The mouth of the righteous is a fountain of life."

Our study of mouths will lead us in a full gospel circle from realistic despair, to real hope. In Part I we commence by being completely overcome by the power and beauty of the mouth of our holy God. As the heavens are higher than the earth so is his mouth bigger, and more powerful than ours. His is a mouth far above all mouths, a mouth we might even think of as magical, except that it belongs to God. Scriptures tell us that as image bearers, our mouths should be little reflections of His mouth.

However, like King David we sense our utter failure in this and cry out for help, "Set a guard over my mouth, O, Lord, keep watch over my lips."Part II of this study concerns training "our guard" to be watchful and diligent.

Part III is about all the things God **does** want our mouths to be used for, all the ways in which our mouths can be, like his, fountains of life.

These "dos and "don'ts "covered in Parts II and III, though very practically instructive and edifying, eventually have the effect of all law – depression and despair. They teach us of our desperate need and lead us to our Savior.

Then, when with our faltering mouths, we confess our complete failure and put our trust in Him, He will give us new hearts. And, full circle, we discover that "out of the overflow of the (new) heart the mouth speaks." Our mouths do become more like His.

What a treasure we humans, made in His image, have in this unique gift of thought and speech, and what a marvel that our mouths can be redeemed and perfected!

And the climax at the end? That's too fine a surprise to allude to in the introduction!

PART I
His Mouth and Ours

Every word of God is flawless."
Proverbs 30:5

"Men will have to give account on the Day of Judgment for every careless
word they have spoken."
Matthew 12:36

Lesson One:
God's Awesome Mouth

Six Breathtaking Characteristics of God's Mouth
Characteristic Number One--

Some people are spectacularly creative. Leonardo da Vinci was one of the most fascinatingly ingenious people history has ever known. We call Leonardo Da Vinci a Renaissance man, or a "polymath" because he was interested in everything and seemed to be skilled at everything. He was an astronomer, sculptor, geologist, mathematician, botanist, animal behaviorist, inventor, engineer, architect and even a musician. Da Vinci came up with hundreds of different inventions. His mind was fertile and he had a remarkable knack for knowing how to get ideas out of his mind, off of his notes, and into some real material form. He was a prolific inventor, but he also left many, if not most, of his inventions unfinished while he caved in to the excitement of his next novel idea. Da Vinci is an example of one of humanity's most imaginative and resourceful men, yet he was far from being a god.

We often have brainy ideas but don't have the time, talent, or resources to fashion our ideas and dreams into realities. We can **think** of paintings that we cannot paint. We can **design** houses that we will never be able to build. We can **imagine** contraptions that are impossible to explain to other people, and might take Leonardo DaVinci a life time to make. Even the most ingenious among us can't just think things and ... puff, they ARE! For us they *ARE* only thoughts. It takes us great amounts of time, energy, and supplies to bring our imaginings into material existence, if it can be done at all.

<u>God, on the other hand, has such an extraordinary mouth, that HE can speak His thoughts into being!</u> **Now <u>that</u> is cool.**

In this lesson we want to try to get some sense of how awe inspiring the mouth of God is, and this is perhaps one of the most remarkable mind-boggling characteristics of His mouth - <u>His words can bring things into existence!</u>

At creation, <u>God's mouth was a virtual fountain of life</u>! Look at Genesis chapter one verses 3,6,9,14,20, 24, and 26.

He said, "Let there be light," and there was light."

He said, "Let there be an expanse..." and it was so.

He said, "Let the land produce vegetation..." and it was so.

"Let the land produce living creatures…" And it was so.

In each instance, God said, "Let there be" and there was!

Incredible! Can you picture Him walking around making His ideas come to life by speaking them? What an astounding mouth! C. S. Lewis tries to help us envision something of what this could have been like in *The Chronicles of Narnia*.

You can read Lewis' idea about what it may have been like to see God creating life by speaking it into being in *The Magician's Nephew,* chapter nine, *The Founding of Narnia*. Lewis makes Aslan sing the Narnian creation to life. Lewis may be way off in his fiction, but we do know that all three person's of the godhead were there and that they were having a good time delighting in each other and in the work of creation and that it was accomplished in this unbelievable way, by speaking things into being.

Thus, the first characteristic of God's mouth is this:

His mouth is "life-giving". His mouth is a creative fountain of life!

Lesson One
Review Questions

What is one of the most extraordinary characteristics of God's mouth, (the characteristic discussed in lesson one.)?

What does it mean to say that God's mouth is "a fountain of Life?"

What is the simple repeating refrain in Genesis chapter one verses 3, 4, 9, 14, 20, 24, and 26?

Memorize

By the word of the LORD were the heavens made, their starry host by the breath of his mouth.

Psalm 33:6

Lesson Two:
God's Awesome Mouth

Six Breathtaking Characteristics of God's Mouth:

Characteristics Two through Six--

The first characteristic of God's mouth that we considered was His mouth as a fountain of life. It brings forth life. Let's look at five other marvelous characteristics of God's mouth:

Characteristic # 2:

God's mouth is powerful! His words ALWAYS accomplish what He says they will.

- *So is my word that goes out from my mouth: It will not return to me empty, but will accomplish what I desire and achieve the purpose for which I sent it.* Isaiah 55:11

God's words are publicly powerful. All men will see it! All men will eventually recognize the power of God's mouth. What He speaks will always come to pass. See Isaiah 40:5.

- *And the glory of the LORD will be revealed, and all mankind together will see it. For the mouth of the LORD has spoken.* Isaiah 40:5

Characteristic # 3:

His mouth (the Bible = God's words) speaks authoritative words.

- *All Scripture is God-breathed and is useful for teaching, rebuking, correcting, and training in righteousness so that the man of God may be thoroughly equipped for every good work.* II Timothy 3:16

- *I tell you the truth, until heaven and earth disappear, not the smallest letter, not the least stroke of a pen; will by any means disappear from the Law until everything is accomplished.* Matthew 5:18

Characteristic # 4:

Out of God's mouth will come the final judgment!

- *In his right hand he held seven stars, and out of his mouth came a sharp double-edged sword. His face was like the sun shining in all its brilliance.* Revelation 1:16

- *Out of his mouth comes a sharp sword with which to strike down the nations....*
  Revelation 19:15

Characteristic # 5:

God's mouth is eternal. What He says is true, and always will be true! It will always stand!

- *The grass withers and the flowers fall, but the word of our God stands for ever."*
  Isaiah 40:8

- *Your word, O LORD, is eternal, it stands firm in the heavens.* Psalm 119:89

Characteristic #6:

God's Mouth is life sustaining. We cannot live, truly live, without His words.

- *He humbled you, causing you to hunger and then feeding you with manna, which
  neither you nor your fathers had known, to teach you that man does not live
  on bread alone but on every word that comes from the mouth of the LORD.*
  Deuteronomy 8:3

Not only does God's mouth speak life into existence, but it sustains life.

These six characteristics of God's mouth give us lots to meditate on. Try to comprehend the BRINGING-FORTH-LIFE, MIGHTY, AUTHORITATIVE, NEVER CHANGING, TRUSTWORTHY, LIFE- SUSTAINING mouth of God! What a wonder!

In upcoming lessons we will see even more fully what an awesome mouth our God has. It's no wonder God says, *"Is not my word like, fire?"* Jeremiah 23:29

A fuller appreciation for God's mouth will make a sturdier foundation for understanding how, in Christ, our mouths can be little reflections of His. It's an exciting thought to aim at having a mouth like His!

Lesson Two
Review Questions

List six remarkable characteristics of God's mouth.

1._____

2._____

3._____

4._____

5._____

6._____

Memorize

So is my word that goes out from my mouth: It will not return to me empty, but will accomplish what I desire and achieve the purpose for which I sent it.

Isaiah 55:11

The grass withers and the flowers fall, but the word of our God stands for ever.

Isaiah 40:8

Lesson Three:
Mouths Like His – The Beautiful Ideal

Influential parts

Have you ever considered what part of your body is the most powerful influential part?

Of course each part is not only precious and valuable, but each part is so unique it is hard to compare their influence. Each part is especially designed by God to accomplish a specific purpose. We need all the parts of our body and suffer greatly when something goes awry with our hearing, our sight, our speech, our legs, or our arms, not to mention kidneys, livers, lungs or hearts.

Many body parts are so significant that without their proper functioning we would die quickly – in some cases immediately. Without the central control of the brain most other body parts would cease functioning. But suppose we are talking about a healthy person whose body is functioning well. There is a small part of our body that wields a disproportionate and surprising amount of clout when it comes to living productive lives.

THE RIGHT TOOL FOR GETTING THE JOB DONE

Imagine a 300 pound set of weights stubbornly cluttering the family room floor where you are about to seat some guests. You try lifting with your two strong arms. It won't budge. You try shoving with your powerful leg muscles. In exasperation you butt the weights with your head. Finally you resort to the use of your tiny mouth. "Hey, Dad could you please bring your hydraulic lift here a moment?"

It is often our mouths that get a difficult job done. They are amazingly versatile: getting help, explaining ideas, comforting, teaching, entertaining, encouraging, changing the course of our lives, changing the course of other people's lives, saving lives, and helping to save souls.

GOD BRINGS SOMETHING IMPORTANT TO OUR ATTENTION

In Job thirty-nine God points out some of the features of various creatures He made and comments to Job on particular strengths that especially delight Him. He takes pleasure in the ostriches' legs and how she can run. He enjoys the strength of the horse. He remarks on the lion's ability to crouch and lie in wait. The flight of hawks and the soaring ability of eagles please him. But when it comes to man the feature God dwells on the most is the mouth. God wants to be sure we recognize the power that is in our tiny mouths.

In fact, that is what James 3:1-5a is all about.

We all stumble in many ways. If anyone is never at fault in what he says, he is a perfect man, able to keep his whole body in check. When we put bits into the mouths of horses to make them obey us, we can turn the whole animal. Or take ships as an example. Although they are so large and are driven by strong winds, they are steered by a very small rudder wherever the pilot wants to go. Likewise the tongue is a small part of the body, but it makes great boasts.

God compares our influential mouths to tiny rudders steering big ships, little bits turning large horses, and minute sparks igniting blazing forest fires. Our tongues have great capacity to accomplish things, for good or for evil. In Proverbs 18:21 God tells us that *"Death and life are in the power of the tongue."*

This kind of power reminds us of God's powerful mouth that we looked at in lessons one and two. Remember how awesome His mouth is? Remember how He spoke creation into being? Because we are made in the image of God, we have mouths like His. He gave us a mind boggling ability to accomplish things with words. Animals do not have this phenomenal capacity to change things with their words. This is part of what it means to be made like God. In a small way our mouths reflect His. We do have powerful mouths, mouths like His, full of amazing potential.

Lesson Three
Review Questions

1. Read James 3:1- 12. To what three things does James compare our tongues?

    _____

    _____

    _____

2. What do these three things all have in common?

3. Paraphrase (re-write in your own words) Proverbs 18:21.

4. What does this kind of power in our tongues remind us of?

5. In what sense are we distinct from other animals God created?

6. Which two verses in Genesis chapter one describe our uniqueness?

7. How does being made *in the image* of God affect our mouths?

Memorize

Or take ships as an example. Although they are so large and are driven by strong winds, they are steered by a very small rudder wherever the pilot wants to go. Likewise the tongue is a small part of the body, but it makes great boasts.

James 3:4-5

Death and life are in the power of the tongue.

Proverbs 18:21

Lesson Four
Mouths Like His – The Sad Reality

Part of what it means to be made in the image of God is that, like Him, we have the ability to communicate. We both have, and can express, thoughts, ideas, and feelings. The ability to speak is an awesome and powerful gift. Our mouths, like God's, are powerful and effective tools on a much smaller scale. They are reflections of His awesome mouth, and yet they differ from His in a very significant way.

Imperfect Reflections

This difference is a sad reality. God's mouth is not only powerful, life- giving, and life-sustaining, it is absolutely flawless. Ours are not. In this sense our mouths fall utterly short of being the reflections of His that they are meant to be.

Consider the perfection of God's mouth.

- ***EVERY WORD OF GOD IS FLAWLESS***. Proverbs 30:5

- *And the words of the LORD are flawless like silver refined in a furnace of clay, purified seven times.* Psalm 12:6

- *As for God, his way is perfect, the word of the LORD is flawless.* Psalm 18:30

God's words are:

- Perfectly true
- Perfectly holy
- Perfectly kind
- Perfectly loving
- Perfectly suitable
- Perfectly righteous
  - Perfectly Perfect

Our mouths were supposed to be like His but aren't.

We Need Major Help

God's mouth is flawless ours is fallen. Our mouths should have been perfect like His. This fact matters a great deal to God. In fact, God tells us He will hold us accountable for every one of our words. Every one of His is perfect, and we will be judged for every single one of ours.

- *But I tell you that men will have to give account on the Day of Judgment for every careless word they have spoken.* Matthew 12:36

Our powerful mouths, little likenesses of His great mouth, are serious business to God. We can't please Him without learning to control our mouths.

- *If anyone considers himself religious and yet does not keep a tight rein on his tongue, he deceives himself and his religion is worthless.* James 1:26

James 3:2 – 12 pictures both the greatness of our mouths, their significance and potential, and also their utter failure to live up to that greatness, their failure to really reflect the mouth of God in whose image we are made.

Consider what a great forest is set on fire by a small spark.   The tongue also is a fire, a world of evil among the parts of the body. It corrupts the whole person, sets the whole course of his life on fire, and is itself set on fire by hell.   All kinds of animals, birds, reptiles and creatures of the sea are being tamed and have been tamed by man, but no man can tame the tongue. It is a restless evil, full of deadly poison.   With the tongue we praise our Lord and Father, and with it we curse men, who have been made in God's likeness.   Out of the same mouth come praise and cursing. My brothers, this should not be.   Can both fresh water and salt water flow from the same spring?   My brothers, can a fig-tree bear olives, or a grapevine bear figs? Neither can a salt spring produce fresh water.   James 3:2-12

We are made in the image of God and blessed with mouths that echo His mouth's unique abilities, but in our sinful nature we fall utterly and pathetically short of having mouths that are flawless like His. God tells us that though we have succeeded at taming all sorts of creatures, no one can tame their tongue. It appears hopeless.

If we are going to give account of every word, if we want to try to have perfect mouths like His, what can we possibly do?

God Gives Us a Practical Suggestion in Proverbs.

God tells us to set a guard by the door of our mouths and train that guard to arrest wrong words.

- *He who guards his mouth and his tongue keeps himself from calamity.* Proverbs 21:23
- *He who guards his lips guards his life, but he who speaks rashly will come to ruin.* Proverbs 13:3

He makes an allusion to this guard in Ephesians,

- *"Do not let any unwholesome talk come out of your mouths, but only what is helpful for building others up according to their needs, that it may benefit those who listen."* Ephesians 4:29

We need to live each day as though we have a guard in front of our mouth. We need to train that guard to refuse passage of words that are not the kind of words that would come from God's mouth. Our guard needs to know what words will bless.

The guard needs to recognize the enemy. We need to train our guard to be both wise and diligent so that only the words that will benefit people listening will make it passed him.

The next twelve lessons make up boot camp for mouth-guards in training, but be forewarned, no guard will be flawless. The means to flawlessness does not lie with us. This truth will crystallize as we study.

Part II, *A Well Trained Guard*, consists of twelve lessons instructing the guards of our mouths to be on the alert for the following enemies.

Lies
Reckless Words
Gossip
Boasting
Angry Words
Divisive Words & Any That Tear Down
Curses and Spoiling the Lord's Name
Loud Obnoxious, Disruptive, and Silly Words
Foolish Words
Complaining and Grumbling Words
Critical Words
Too-Many-Words

Studying the types of words that we need to guard against reveals what a monumental job it is to make our mouths more like God's mouth. As we study through Part II we will find that the more we consider the task of guarding the door of our mouths, the more overwhelming it grows. We will taste the hopelessness reflected in James 3, and realize that it is impossible to train a guard for ourselves.

David felt this way too. God told us to set a guard over our sinful mouths. But we are weak and helpless. As we consider the task, like David, we respond to God by asking him to help us with this big job!

With David we pray:

Set a guard over my mouth, O LORD; keep watch over the door of my lips.
Psalms 141:3

Lesson Four
Review Questions

1. Our mouths reflect a little of the powerful capabilities of God's but they are very unlike His mouth in another basic way. His mouth is _____, and ours is _____.

2. Matthew 12:36 tells us that one day we will have to give account for (be responsible for) _____.

3. Proverbs makes a suggestion about how we can develop mouths that are more like His. We need to have a _____ by the door of our mouth.

Memorize

Every word of God is flawless.

Proverbs 30:5

Set a guard over my mouth, O LORD; keep watch over the door of my lips.

Psalms 141:3

PART II
A Well Trained Guard

"Set a guard over my mouth, O LORD, keep watch over
the door of my lips."
Psalm 141:3

Introduction to Part II

Summary of Part I   His Mouth and Ours

God has an awesome, creative, life-giving, life-sustaining mouth that is powerful beyond our imagination. His words are eternal. His words are flawless. His mouth is a fountain of life.

Our mouths are made in his imagine. God goes to a lot of trouble to tell us how significant our mouths are. Like His, they are powerful - in an infinitely smaller way. Our tongues have the power of life and death in them. The potential of our mouths is amazing. But our mouths are fallen not flawless. If we want mouths that better reflect His we need to set a guard at the door of our lips and we need to train that guard to recognize which words should be forbidden to pass and arrested. Every word of God's is flawless and we will give an account for every word of ours.

Introduction to Part II   A Well Trained Guard

Part II of this course is something like a boot camp. The next twelve lessons will be rigorous training for the guards of our mouths. We will instruct and drill in each type of speech that needs to be seized at the gate of our mouths and not allowed passage. We'll train our guards to be awake and alert. They will be well informed. We will attempt to train our guards to be so familiar with the enemy words, (all speech that is displeasing to God) until not a word of them will be able to sneak passed no matter how cleverly disguised or deceptive their tactics. At least that's our training goal.

We'll train our guards to be awake, alert, and well informed.

Lesson Five
Imprison Ugly Lies

Four Reasons Why We Should Not Lie

> 1. **Pour and Perish.**

Sometimes people develop a habit of lying for very little reason and of lying freely and often. They do not hesitate. They become habitual liars. They do not allow their consciences to develop. They deny the reality of God hating lies. Sometimes even believers let this part of our old man flourish unchecked. Do we live day by day pouring out lies as though truth and falsehood do not matter? God says He will not tolerate this lack of distinction between truth and falsehood. Those who pour out lies will perish.

- *A false witness will not go unpunished and he who pours out lies will perish.* Proverbs 19:9

> **2. Lies make bad hiding places and we have a truly great hiding place.**

Ever try to hide in a lie? Ever make up a story to hide in so you won't have to face some trouble or the frightening consequences of mistakes you made? Lies don't make very good hiding places. They are often see-through hiding places. We look like a toddler playing hide-and-seek behind a post that he unknowingly sticks out of on either side. Lies are also bad hiding places because they get uncovered. Someone will come in and pull the blanket off the couch. Oops. Lies are uncertain places to hide in. They don't feel safe. They feel sickening and scary.

Why hide in a lie when we have such a wonderful hiding place in God? He invites us to hide in Him. If we run to Him when we are in trouble and ask for His help to deal with the situation He will shelter us and do with us what is ultimately for our best good. His arms are marvelous and safe. He is our refuge in time of trouble.

- ***For we have made a lie our refuge and falsehood our hiding place.*** *So this is what the Sovereign LORD says: 'See I lay a stone in Zion, a tested stone, a precious cornerstone for a sure foundation; the one who trusts will never be dismayed. I will make justice the measuring line and righteousness the plumb line.* ***Hail will sweep away your refuge, the lie, and water will overflow your hiding place….*** Isaiah 28:15

And then at the closing of Chapter 28 we read,

- *All this also comes from the LORD Almighty wonderful in counsel and magnificent in wisdom.*

What a tremendous place to run in times of trouble! In this hiding place we will find God's magnificent wisdom. His justice and righteousness will be applied to the situation. He tells us we will not be dismayed. Such a contrast to hiding in a lie! Tempted to lie? Run to Him. Hide in Him.

3. We are members one of another.

It is utter foolishness for us to lie to one another as believers because we are one body. We are to take off the old man and put on Christ. Falsehood is a part of our old man. We are new creations in Christ and we are joined together with each other. We do not need to lie to each other. We do not need to fear each other or earn each other's respect. We have it already because we are one in Christ. So we tell each other the truth.

- *Therefore, putting away falsehood, let everyone speak the truth with his neighbor, for we are members one of another.* Ephesians 4:25

4. Lies made His top ten.

When God chose just ten commands to give to His people to show them who He was and what His nature required of them, telling the truth made it into the TOP TEN. It is a fundamental basic truth that God is truth, and He loves the truth. It is part of who God is. He included it in the Ten Commandments.

- *You shall not give false testimony against your neighbor.* Exodus 20:16

How Ugly is Ugly? Four Indications of its Ugliness:

1. Lies made His top six twice!

How ugly are lies? God hates them. God talks a lot about lies and liars in the Bible. It is very obvious that he hates lies. In Proverbs 6:16-19 God lists six things that he particularly hates. He detests these things. Lying makes it into this special-mention-list twice!

2. Satan is the father of lies.

How ugly are lies? As ugly as the devil! Jesus tells us that Satan is the father of lies.

Referring to Satan in John 8:44 Jesus says,

- *For there is no truth in him. When he lies, he speaks his native language, for he is a liar and the father of lies.*

When we lie, we are speaking Satan's native language. Nothing helps bond us to someone as readily as learning to speak their mother tongue! Lying is a sober matter.

3. Liars belong in a bad group and are dealt with as all in the group are.

- *But the cowardly, the unbelieving, the vile, the murderers, the sexually immoral, those who practice magic arts, the idolaters and all liars—their place will be in the fiery lake of burning sulfur. This is the second death.* Revelation 21:8

- *Outside are the dogs, those who practice magic arts, the sexually immoral, the murderers, the idolaters and everyone who loves and practices falsehood.* Revelation 22:15

4. Get the picture – Truth is part of God's very nature. He hates deception and falsehood!

To take the truth lightly is to ignore God.

Just listen to His word on the subject:

- Proverbs 12:22 – *"The LORD detests lying lips, but he delights in men who are truthful."*

- Psalm 101:7 – *"No one who practices deceit will dwell in my house; no one who speaks falsely will stand in my presence."*

- Psalm 5:4 – *"The arrogant cannot stand in your presence; you hate all who do wrong. You destroy those who tell lies; bloodthirsty and deceitful men the Lord abhors."*

- Proverbs 30:8 – *"Keep falsehood and lies far from me…"*

- Romans 3:13 *"There is no one who does good not even one. Their throats are open graves, their tongues practice deceit… there is no fear of God before their eyes."*

Truth is an integral part of who God is. That is what makes falsehood and lies so horrible. We need to understand of how heinous anything deceptive is.

Why Do We Lie?

Sometimes when we are trying to break a habit, it's helpful to recognize the kind of situations that cause us to indulge in that habit. It can help us see more clearly what might push us to do what we do not want to do. In a sermon John Piper once described two kinds of fear and two kinds of greed that tempt us to lie.

- The fear of losing self esteem
- The fear of physical harm
&
- The greed for praise
- The greed for money and things

What tempts us to lie?
• To avoid punishment
• To avoid conflict
• To avoid hurting someone else
• To avoid hurting someone else's feelings
• To avoid having to face unpleasant truths about ourselves
• To avoid having to admit mistakes we made
• To gain power
• To gain admiration or respect
• To gain money or material goods

Satan gets us to lie by lying to us about what is truly desirable. He gets us to think that someone's opinion of us is more important than telling the truth or that physical safety is more desirable than the truth. We need to believe and trust in who God is. If we know the truth about God's goodness and sovereignty we won't have to distort the truth in order to get things or money or praise or respect. We can leave this in His hands. **Telling the truth is a matter of trusting God and resting in his goodness.**

John Piper: *"The lies of Satan that beget lies of sinners have to be replaced by the truth of Jesus that begets truthfulness of saints."*

THE ULTIMATE LIE AND THE ULTIMATE HOPE FOR LIARS

Who is the ultimate liar? It is the man who denies that Jesus is the Christ! (I John 2:22)

Paul tells us in Romans one that the problem people have is that they have exchanged the truth of God for a lie. In our sinful nature lying comes natural to us and it cuts us off from God.

Thank God for giving us hope. Because Jesus died for us we can be forgiven of all our ugly lies. When God draws us to Himself and we confess Christ with our mouth, God gives us a new heart. We are clean and forgiven. God enables us to see the truth through Christ. We love Him and we desire to please Him. We hate falsehood because He hates it and we love the truth because He loves the truth.

- *Do not lie to each other, since you have taken off your old self with its practices and have put on the new self, which is being renewed in knowledge in the image of its Creator.* Colossians 3:9

Jesus' Mouth, the Image of God's Invisible Mouth

Peter tells us in I Peter 2:21-22
"To this you were called, because Christ suffered for you, leaving you an example, that you should follow in his steps. "He committed no sin, and no deceit was found in his mouth."

The new me, my new self, will be conforming to the image of my Creator's mouth by giving up lies, because there was no deceit in Jesus' mouth.

Mouth Guard Boot Camp Exercises 1-3
How to Deal with Lies

Help Jack and Jill Out of These Terrible Fixes.

Exercise 1

Jill is a Christian and she has been telling other kids in her Physical Science class at school about God. Some of them are interested. A bunch of them know about her faith. Last week the teacher in that class assigned a report on the green house effect. All week Jill was busy helping her mother clean house and get ready for company that was coming to stay for a whole month! They had to move around furniture in two rooms. She did not get a chance to work on her report. She has barely started it.

This morning the reports were due. Everyone was supposed to put their report on Ms. Stinkles desk at the beginning of class. Everyone did. Except Jill. Ms. Stinkle, who thinks very highly of Jill and knows she is a diligent student, just asked Jill, in front of the whole class, "Where is *your* report, Jill? I'm sure you did it, but I don't see it here?"

Jill is mortified. All sorts of things flash through Jill's mind. She is afraid Ms. Stinkle will think she is making up the story about cleaning house for her mother. She also knows that that is not really an excuse for not doing the report. She does not want to ruin her good reputation. Then she remembers how many people in that class know she is a Christian. She doesn't want to ruin their impression of Christians by admitting that she is not such a responsible student after all. She thinks quickly to herself, "I'll just tell her I **did** put it on her desk and it must have gotten lost. Then I'll stay up tonight and write it really fast and give her another copy tomorrow and pretend it is the second one I am giving her. Then nobody will lose respect for me or God."

"What?" she replied in a shocked voice, "I put it on top of the other papers on your desk this morning. It should be there."

"How strange," responded Ms. Stinkle with at quizzical twist of her eyebrows, "I'll look through the stack again."

----

1. What SHOULD Jill have said to Ms. Stinkle instead of resorting to a lie? Give two examples of what she might have said.

2. Now that the lie has been told what should Jill do or say?

Exercise 2

Jack's dad is really into being good stewards of the bodies God has given us. P.E. is the only part of home school Dad is involved in this year. Every single day for weeks now when Dad gets home from work he has been asking, "Jack, did you do your calisthenics and aerobics?" Sometimes when Jack admits that he wasn't able to get around to it Dad has made him drop everything and go do them right then and there.

Today Jack worked hard on school work all day. He caught up in Algebra (from being three whole lessons behind!) and he wrote a long history report besides all his other subjects. He was really proud of all he got done and excited to tell Dad about his accomplishments. Jack worked that hard partly because he has wanted to watch *The Return of King* which everyone else but him got to see two weeks ago. He knew he would have to start watching the long movie by six-thirty or mom and dad would tell him it couldn't be done on a school night. Jack had managed a minor miracle and was pretty psyched. He was all set up with everything accomplished that had to be done and he was looking forward to melting into the comfortable brown leather chair and pushing that remote button for what he knew would be the best movie he had ever seen.

Dad drove up. Jack was excited to meet him and tell him how well the day had gone. Dad stepped in the door and set his brief case on the kitchen table. "Hi, Jack, How's it going? Did you do your calisthenics and aerobics today?"

Jack's heart sank! Drat! The one thing he forgot, or just didn't get to after all that hard work, and Dad had to greet him with that. He felt so frustrated and sick. What difference would it make if he just said a quick "Yep." He **did do** them **almost every** day.
What would it matter to miss this once? If he said "No," Dad would start lecturing or tell him to go do them now and everything he had worked so hard toward all day long would be wasted.

"Yep" he beamed.

"Good job." Dad beamed back.

Jack didn't bother to tell his dad all the other things he had been so excited about.

1. What SHOULD Jack have said to his dad instead of resorting to a lie? Give two examples of what he might have said.

2. Now that the lie has been told what should Jack do or say?

Exercise 3

Klondike bars are Jill's favorite ice cream bars. Her family doesn't buy them very often but once in a while on a special occasion Mom gets a box of them. There are six in the box. Since Mom is perpetually on a diet and doesn't eat one, and there are four kids and one dad, there is always one Klondike bar left in the box after they are served. This is a bad situation.

Jill has been very frustrated with her little brother for always helping himself to that extra one the next day. Last time she scolded him and called him "a little pig" for being so greedy. "You should at least ask Mom before you take it, you little pig," she had said, "That is the rule around here you know."

"Yeah, like you keep all the rules." Her brother taunted.

"I do," thought Jill. And she usually did.

Last night Jill's family had Klondike bars. Today is Saturday and everyone in the family has been doing chores all morning; mowing, weeding, painting the deck, trimming bushes. It's hot and they are all sweaty. Jill's brothers and sisters all came in and had their lunch while she was painting the last railing on the deck. She wanted to finish up before lunch but they were all hungry so Mom told them to go ahead and eat and Jill could finish the deck and get lunch when she was done.

When Jill came in for her lunch she was really hot and tired. She ate her tuna sandwich and went to the fridge to get a piece of cool water melon. She could hardly believe her eyes when she saw the empty platter. They hadn't left her even one slice of water melon. She was so disappointed. She had been imagining that cool water melon on her tongue to get herself through the last minutes of the tiresome paint job. She scrounged around the fridge. Nothing in there that looked refreshing. She pulled open the freezer. There was that last Klondike bar. That would be an even trade off for the watermelon she had missed out on. She got it out and went out in the hammock to eat it.

Later that afternoon Mom and all the kids were gathered in the kitchen working on some applesauce. The Fizzywig family was in the living room having their Bible study with Dad. Their fussy little toddler was carrying on and preventing Mrs. Fizzywig from paying attention to the study. Mom noticed. "Oh, Jill, will you get out that Klondike bar from last night? I was saving that to keep little Bonny happy with during the study."

Jill was confused and fumbled around in the freezer while she thought what to say. She recalled with chagrin how she had scolded her brother for helping himself without asking. She almost always asked in such instances, but she hadn't this time. He would be sure to point out how hypocritical she was. Why should she get in trouble for doing something when she was almost always so good? "I don't see it in here, Mom" she stuttered with her head still in the freezer. That wasn't a lie.

"That's odd. Who ate that bar?' Mom inquired.

A chorus of four "not me"s filled the kitchen and Mom let out a long sad sigh.

---

1.   What should Jill have said when her mom asked for the Klondike bar?

2.   What should Jill do or say now that the lie came out?

Lesson Five
Review Questions

1. What is the number one ugly heinous enemy the guard of our mouth should look for and deal with? _____

2. What are two types of fears and two types of greed that often tempt us to lie?

   _____   _____

   _____   _____

3. What happens to those who "pour out lies"?

4. What problems are there with hiding behind lies? Where should we hide when we are in a difficult situation?

5. What reason does Ephesians 4:25 give us for not lying?

6. Who is the father of lies?

7. With whom does God group liars?

8. Briefly describe God's attitude towards deception.

9. What is THE ultimate lie?

10. What hope is there for liars?

Memorize

The LORD detests lying lips, but he delights in men who are truthful.
Proverbs 12:22

Lesson Six
Arrest Reckless Words

Ok, I'm watching out for those heinous lies. I won't let a lie get through these lips. Now what else do you want me to do?

God knows everything. He is never missing a piece of information. God has thought long and hard about all His holy will. It is established, firm, and never changing. He has a perfect plan based on all His wisdom and knowledge and holiness. God's words are flawless partly because they are never reckless. Everything HE speaks is part of His wise plan.

We, on the other hand, know very little. We frequently speak without knowing what we are talking about. Our plans and ideas are not wisely and carefully laid before we open our mouths. We hear something and respond to it in a flash before we understand the situation. Our words are rash. They are foolish because we do not have knowledge before we speak them. They are careless because we have not cared enough to understand before we speak. When we speak recklessly without first taking the time to consider the situation and look to God for wisdom to say the right thing, our words are like a sword piercing the one we speak to. Reckless words are something else we need to guard against.

Here's what God says about them.

- *Reckless words pierce like a sword, but the tongue of the wise brings healing.* Proverbs 12:18

- *He who answers before listening – that is his folly and his shame.* Proverbs 18:13

- *Do you see a man who speaks in haste? There is more hope for a fool than for him.* Proverbs 29:20

- *But I tell you that men will have to give account on the Day of Judgment for every careless word they have spoken.* Matthew 12:36

We should force ourselves to stop and think before we speak. Often we should pray before we speak. We need to practice holding back words until we are certain we understand the situation and have considered what the most helpful response would be.

A Biblical Story about Reckless Words

Esau

There are several stories in the Bible that illustrate the folly and damage of reckless words. One of the most well-known of these stories tells us something about the consequences of reckless words. It is the story of Esau selling his birth right for a bowl of lentil stew recounted in Genesis 25:27-34.

The boys grew up, and Esau became a skillful hunter, a man of the open country, while Jacob was content to stay at home among the tents. Isaac, who had a taste for wild game, loved Esau, but Rebekah loved Jacob.
Once when Jacob was cooking some stew, Esau came in from the open country, famished. He said to Jacob, "Quick, let me have some of that red stew! I'm famished!" (That is why he was also called Edom.)
Jacob replied, "First sell me your birthright."
"Look, I am about to die," Esau said. "What good is the birthright to me?"
But Jacob said, "Swear to me first." So he swore an oath to him, selling his birthright to Jacob.
Then Jacob gave Esau some bread and some lentil stew. He ate and drank, and then got up and left.
So Esau despised his birthright.

The book of Hebrews reveals the consequences of Esau's reckless words, "Look I'm about to die. What good is the birthright to me?"

Hebrews 12:16-17 says:
"See that no one is sexually immoral, or is godless like Esau, who for a single meal sold his inheritance rights as the oldest son. Afterward, as you know, when he wanted to inherit this blessing, he was rejected. Even though he sought the blessing with tears, he could not change what he had done."

"Even though he sought the blessing with tears, he could not change what he had done." is a common experience for us when we have spoken reckless words. Words simply cannot be taken back no matter how earnestly we wish to retract them. Once out they are out and reckless ones have caused irrevocable damage. A tube of toothpaste provides a good illustration of the irrevocable nature of our words once out of our mouths. It's so easy to squeeze the toothpaste out but so difficult to stuff it back in.

Jesus' Mouth, the Image of God's Invisible Mouth

Jesus, the image of the invisible God, provides our ultimate look at the mouth of God. In everything aspect of what we study about our mouths, we will look at Jesus' mouth to see what our mouths, mouths made in His image and now being redeemed and restored to that image bearing, should be like. Did Jesus avoid reckless words?

Some might argue that He indulged in them. "You Vipers!" His words were sometimes bold and even outrageous. He called the Pharisees vipers on a number of occasions. But bold shocking language can be helpful. When Jesus spoke that way it was not off the cuff It was not without thought or care. On the contrary the Bible paints a picture of a Messiah that avoids reckless words even in the most goading of circumstances. The famous passage in Isaiah 53:7 points to Christ's complete victory over the temptation to speak reckless words even under the greatest of provocation!

"He was oppressed and afflicted, yet he did not open his mouth; he was led like a lamb to the slaughter, and as a sheep before its shearers is silent, so he did not open his mouth."

In the gospels we see this prophetic description of our Savior borne out. Even in a moment of extreme vexation, even when his words could have saved his life, Jesus did not open His mouth and respond with the kind of reckless words anyone of us would have.

When he was accused by the chief priests and the elders, he gave no answer. Then Pilate asked him, "Don't you hear the testimony they are bringing against you?" But Jesus made no reply, not even to a single charge—to the great amazement of the governor. Matthew 27:12-13

Again in the Gospel of Mark 14:57-61 Mark testifies to Jesus' complete avoidance of reckless words.
"Then some stood up and gave this false testimony against him: "We heard him say, 'I will destroy this temple made with human hands and in three days will build another, not made with hands.'" Yet even then their testimony did not agree. Then the high priest stood up before them and asked Jesus, "Are you not going to answer? What is this testimony that these men are bringing against you?" But Jesus remained silent and gave no answer."

I Peter 2:23 describes for us how it was that Jesus avoided reckless words. *"When they hurled their insults at him, he did not retaliate; when he suffered, he made no threats. Instead, he entrusted himself to him who judges justly."* Jesus was able to resist retaliating with reckless words because he knew that His Father would judge justly. He knew God would make all things right. Esau could not even bare a rumbling stomach without resorting to reckless words. What a contrast we see in Christ who suffered insults and threats and injustice and unthinkable pain all while laying down His birth right for us.

Jesus teaches us that to avoid reckless words we need to meditate on God's justice, kindness and ultimate sovereignty over all things. This is our Savior. He went silently to be slaughtered for us, that we might be set free from slavery to our sinful mouths that are so ready with reckless words. He lived without sin, holy before God, a suitable sacrifice. He lived out a perfect example for us and died to free us to follow that example. May God give us mouths like His, mouths that speak no reckless words.

Mouth Guard Boot Camp Exercises
Arresting Reckless Words

For each of these situations imagine what reckless words you might speak? Then imagine what the situation might really have been had you taken the time and effort to understand before you spoke? The hope is that this exercise in imagination might serve as a reminder when we are faced with a temptation to respond with reckless words. There might just be something we need to stop and realize before we open our mouths.

1. You come home from a soccer game. You are tired and really hungry for that lasagna dinner your mom promised you tonight, but when you go into the kitchen you see leftovers on the table, ones you really didn't like the first time around.

What might your reckless words be?

What explanation might you have missed?

2. Your sister runs into the living room when dad calls for family worship. She plops down on the couch beside you. She smells really bad.

What might your reckless words be?

What explanation might you have missed?

3. Your sister has been in the bathroom for at least 30 minutes. You have been trying to be patient but you are getting late and really need to get in there.

What might your reckless words be?

What explanation might you have missed?

4. You have been saving money for two months now. As far as you know no one knows where you have it stashed away. You open the door of your bedroom and there is your older brother sitting on the floor counting out **your** hidden money!

What might your reckless words be?

What explanation might you have missed?

Hopefully these funny exercises will serve as helpful reminders for us. Often we need to stop and find out the story behind a situation. But these four silly examples of situations that need to be thoughtfully understood before we respond are not the only type of situations in which we will need to avoid speaking reckless words. Sometimes we stop before speaking, but there is no helpful explanation even when we take the time to find out. Sometimes what we have to remember before speaking is not a funny twist that will be revealed. Sometimes we just need to stop and remember that God is just and entrust ourselves to Him. We need to recall that words cannot be stuffed back in the tube. We do not want to have bitter regrets for our reckless words like Esau had.

To avoid reckless words, remember:
- **The Cause** = answering before listening. Speaking too fast without taking the time to think first.
- **The Result** = hurt people (pierced like a sword pierces)
- **The Means of Prevention** = Stop. Listen. Consider. Hold back until you understand the situation well, and remember the bottom line - God is just. We do not need to stand up for everything ourselves. He will make it all right.

Lesson Six
Review Questions

1. According to Proverbs 18:13, what causes reckless rash words?

2. According to Proverbs 12:18, what is often the result of reckless rash words?

3. What is a simple remedy for preventing reckless words?

4. What did Jesus remember that helped Him avoid reckless words?

Memorize

Reckless words pierce like a sword, but the tongue of the wise brings healing.
Proverbs 12:18

Lesson Seven
Confine Gossip

The words of a talebearer (a gossiper) are as wounds, and they go down into the innermost parts of the belly. Proverbs 18:8

> What is gossip?

The Hebrew word that we translate as "gossip" in the Old Testament means, "one who reveals secrets, one who goes about as a talebearer or scandal-monger."

If we have special access to private information about someone and we reveal it to other people who do not need to know it, we are gossiping. Gossip is speaking of the faults or failures of other people, telling about shameful embarrassing details of their lives without their permission to do so. Sometimes the information we share is true and accurate, but still gossip, other times the information is not even true and we are carelessly passing it on without verifying it ourselves. In this instance we are both lying (if in our laziness or cowardliness, we did not bother to discern the truth) and gossiping, because even if it were true the person we are talking to does not need to know about it.

In short, gossip is communication that hurts people. Gossip in another type of speech that the guards of our mouths need to watch for. It should not be allowed to come through our lips.

Why do we gossip?

- Often we share the information because we have either a conscious or unconscious desire to make ourselves look good by making someone else look bad.

- Sometimes we gossip just to show off the fact that we are important enough to have this special information.

- Sometimes we just have not carefully considered how harmful our sharing of secrets will be.

What are the Effects of Gossip?

- Gossip destroys trust. (See Proverbs 11:12)
- Gossip separates friends. (See Proverbs 16:28 and 17:9)
- Gossip causes deadly wounds. (See Proverbs 18:8 and 26:22)
- Gossip causes strife. (See Proverbs 26:20)
- Gossip causes dissension. (See Proverbs 6:19)
- Gossip has even led to murder. (Psalms 31:13 and Ezekiel 22:9)

"The words of a talebearer are as wounds, and they go down into the innermost parts of the belly" Proverbs 18:8

It topples governments, wrecks marriages, destroys friendships, devastates loved ones, ruins careers, busts reputations, causes heartaches, nightmares, indigestion, spawns suspicion, generates grief, dispatches innocent people to cry in their pillows.

Even its name hisses. It's called gossip.

Office gossip. Shop gossip. Party gossip. School gossip. Church gossip.

It makes headlines and headaches.

Before you repeat a story, ask yourself:

Is it true?
Is if fair?
Is it necessary?

If not, be quiet!
(Author unknown)

What Does God Have to Say about Gossip?

Gossip is serious sin.

The ninth Commandment, "You shall not bear false witness against your neighbor" Exodus 20:16, focuses on the harm done to one's neighbor.

God, in the book of James, explains: "Do not speak evil of one another, brethren. He who speaks evil of a brother and judges his brother, speaks evil of the law and judges the law. But if you judge the law, you are not a doer of the law but a judge" James 4:11. Gossiping is bearing false witness, which apart from the grace offered in the gospel, deserves the death penalty. Romans 6:23.

Furthermore, we can see the seriousness of gossip in the book of Romans. Paul includes gossips and slanderers in the list of sins that have provoked God's wrath. Romans 1:29b-32. We see from this passage how serious the sin of gossip is and that it characterizes those who are under God's wrath.

Many other passages in scripture also teach us of God's serious attitude toward gossip.

Leviticus 19:16 – *"Do not go about spreading slander among your people. Do not do anything that endangers your neighbor's life. I am the Lord."*

Proverbs 11:13 – *"A gossip betrays a confidence, but a trustworthy man keeps a secret."*

Romans 1:29 – *"They have become filled with every kind of wickedness, evil, greed and depravity. They are full of envy, murder, strife, deceit and malice. They are gossips."*

1 Timothy 5:13 – *"Besides, they get into the habit of being idle and going about from house to house. And not only do they become idlers, but also gossips and busybodies, saying things they ought not to."*

Matthew 7:1 – *"Do not judge, or you too will be judged."*

Proverbs 18:8 – *"The words of gossip are like choice morsels; they go down to a man's inmost parts."*

God's warnings about gossip are so serious that it might be a helpful practice to imagine ourselves with a knife in hand, stabbing the person we are about to slander each time we are tempted to gossip. This would help us see the sober reality of what we are doing.

God wants us to realize how awful gossip is. Gossip slanders a neighbor. It destroys a person's character or personal reputation. God warns us that he who lives by the sword of slander shall die by the sword of slander. He says,

"Whoever secretly slanders his neighbor, him I will destroy" Psalm 101:5.

It is critically important that we train the guard of our mouth to stop gossip. How can we train them to recognize gossip and catch it every time?

How can we train our mouth guards to detect gossip?

Gossip Detection Procedure:

To stop gossip, we must recognize it. But how?

God has laid out a gossip-detection procedure in Philippians 4:8.

Step 1: It must be *true*. "Prove all things; hold fast that which is good." I Thessalonians 5:21. Deuteronomy 13:14 says, "Then you must inquire, probe and investigate it thoroughly." If something negative about another person can't be proven, it shouldn't be listened to or spoken of.

Step 2: It must be *noble*. Even if something is true, we might still do better to refrain from sharing it if it is not noble. We should not tarnish the character, name or reputation of another person. Any hint of disrespect should set off an alarm in our mind that shouts "Gossip!"

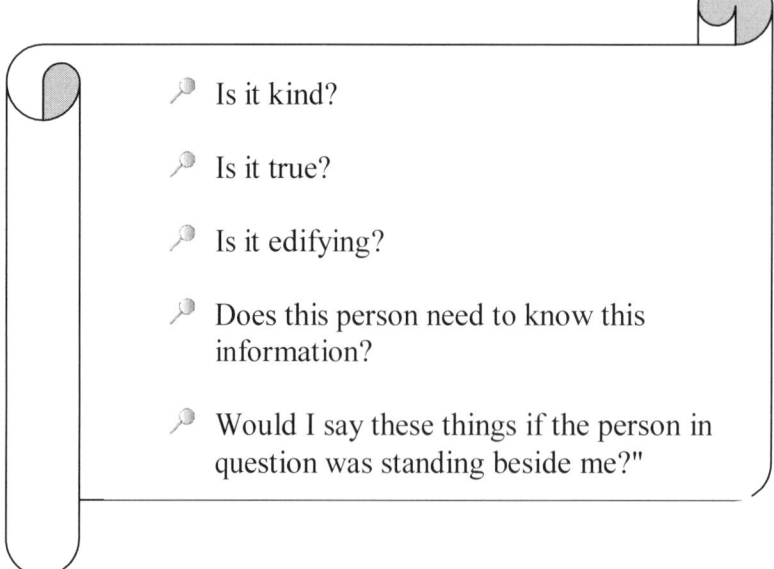 **Step 3: It must be *just*.** Paul declares that the information must be *just*. This means we should not discuss the sins of others. "For all have sinned and fall short of the glory of God," he says in Romans 3:23. "He who covers a transgression seeks love, but he who repeats a matter separates the best of friends" Proverbs 17:9

Step 4: It must be *pure*. Another important part of our gossip detection procedure is *purity*. The words must be *pure*. God does not want His people listening to or spreading dirty words or stories. Keep your ears and mouth pure.

Step 5: It must be *lovely*. Accept only *lovely* things into your mind ---- things that effect you and others in a positive, uplifting way and let only those come out of your mouth. .

Step 6: It must be a *good report*. Bad news bombards us constantly. Human nature seems to thrive on bad news. "For their heart devises violence, and their lips talk of troublemaking" Paul tells us to avoid bad reports.

Use the gossip detectors: truth, honor, righteousness, purity, loveliness and good reports to guard against gossip.

Another handy field guide for identifying gossip on the fly is this simple set of questions. Always make it your practice to ask yourself:

- Is it kind?

- Is it true?

- Is it edifying?

- Does this person need to know this information?

- Would I say these things if the person in question was standing beside me?"

What is the opposite of gossip and serves as an antidote to it?

The antidote to gossip is speaking about good things, praising, encouraging, and building others up. Make this what you do instead! If you want to avoid gossip, focus on creating helpful and encouraging statements.

If you refuse to gossip, your decision might be what brings about the end of a very painful ordeal.
Proverbs 26:20 – "Without wood a fire goes out; without gossip a quarrel dies down."

We should remember how much gossip hurts us when we are the victims of it, and be sure to treat others the way we would want to be treated. Matthew 7:12 – *"So in everything, do to others what you would have them do to you, for this sums up the Law and the Prophets."*

Instead of gossip, speak words of *praise* ---- Speak words of praise about the good in people. Encourage others to do their best. Comfort people when they are discouraged.

In short, use your tongue to bring life ---- not death! Let your mouth be a reflection of His life giving mouth.

Jesus' Mouth, the Image of God's Invisible Mouth

Jesus gave His disciples another means of avoiding gossip, something He obviously did himself. In addition to speaking words of praise, encouragement, and comfort Jesus taught His disciples to avoid gossip by speaking directly to the sinful person involved instead of talking to other people about them.

In Matthew 18:15-16   Jesus teaches His disciples:
"If your brother or sister sins, go and point out their fault, just between the two of you. If they listen to you, you have won them over. But if they will not listen, take one or two others along, so that 'every matter may be established by the testimony of two or three witnesses.

Jesus never hesitated to directly confront one of His disciples when they needed it. No where do we see Jesus talking to one disciple about another's fault, or even another's story. He was much more apt to give an Aslan-like reply telling one disciple that the other's story was nothing he had to hear. Jesus taught us how to avoid gossip. Speak <u>to</u> people, not <u>about</u> people.

Lesson Seven
Review Questions

1. Define Gossip.

2. What are the steps in the gossip detection process? (What questions can the guards of our mouths ask about words that are coming out of our mouths to determine if they are gossip?)

3. What serves as a beautiful antidote to gossip, the better way, the way to use our mouths to bring life, not death?

Memorize:

A gossip betrays a confidence, but a trustworthy man keeps a secret.

Proverbs 11:13

Lesson Eight
Incarcerate Boasting

The next enemy we need to train the guards of our mouths to look out for is boasting.

To boast is to speak with exaggeration and pride usually about oneself. It is self praise about a particular ability or possession. Sometimes boasting is making bold pronouncements about something we are planning to accomplish.

Boasting is an ugly sin. It is a pathetic effort to steal the glory that belongs to God or, on a human level, the attention and appreciation that belongs to others.

Psalm 94:4

> *They pour out arrogant words; all the evildoers are full of boasting.*

What's wrong with boasting?

Basically three things should keep us from boasting.

1. We do not know what the final word on anything is. The end of the matter is hidden from us. We don't know who will win tomorrow. We are too ignorant and in the dark to be able to boast.

James 4:13-16

> *Now listen, you who say, "Today or tomorrow we will go to this or that city, spend a year there, carry on business and make money." Why, you do not even know what will happen tomorrow. What is your life? You are a mist that appears for a little while and then vanishes. Instead, you ought to say, "If it is the Lord's will, we will live and do this or that." As it is, you boast and brag. All such boasting is evil.*

Proverbs 27:1

> *Do not boast about tomorrow, for you do not know what a day may bring forth.*

2. God tells us that praise should come from others, not ourselves.

Proverbs 27:2

Let another praise you, and not your own mouth; someone else, and not your own lips.

3. Boasting is completely inappropriate because God is our all in all. All things come from Him, including all our gifts. We are nothing at all in ourselves! All our boasting should be in Him. All glory belongs to Him. Our hearts desire should be to see Him glorified not ourselves.

Jeremiah 9:23

This is what the LORD says:
   "Let not the wise man boast of his wisdom
   or the strong man boast of his strength
   or the rich man boast of his riches,

Isaiah 10:15
Does the ax raise itself above him who swings it,
   or the saw boast against him who uses it?
   As if a rod were to wield him who lifts it up,
   or a club brandish him who is not wood!

Romans chapter 3 makes it clear how inappropriate boasting is. We are all sinners without any hope apart from God's mercy. We have nothing of our own to boast in!

There is no one righteous, not even one…

Now we know that whatever the law says, it says to those who are under the law, so that every mouth may be silenced and the whole world held accountable to God…

But now a righteousness from God, apart from law, has been made known, to which the Law and the Prophets testify. This righteousness from God comes through faith in Jesus Christ to all who believe. There is no difference, for all have sinned and fall short of the glory of God, and are justified freely by his grace through the redemption that came by Christ Jesus. God presented him as a sacrifice of atonement, through faith in his blood. He did this to demonstrate his justice, because in his forbearance he had left the sins committed beforehand unpunished—he did it to demonstrate his justice at the present time, so as to be just and the one who justifies those who have faith in Jesus.

Where, then, is boasting? It is excluded.

Galatians 6:14

   May I never boast except in the cross of our Lord Jesus Christ, through which the world has been crucified to me, and I to the world.

Who tends to be boastful?

1. Little children

"Look at me! I can swing higher than you can."

"I can jump higher than you."

"I have more Legos than you do!"

"I can eat four hot dogs. You only ate two."

"I have my own cell phone."

"I got my permit on my 15'th birthday."

2. Military officers and politicians boast freely today and have done so throughout history.

Think of King Sennacherib.

The field commander said to them, "Tell Hezekiah, " 'This is what the great king, the king of Assyria, says: On what are you basing this confidence of yours? 2 Kings 18:19

Isaiah 10:8-15

Are not my commanders all kings?' he says.

Has not Calno fared like Carchemish?
Is not Hamath like Arpad,
and Samaria like Damascus?

As my hand seized the kingdoms of the idols,
kingdoms whose images excelled those of Jerusalem and Samaria-

shall I not deal with Jerusalem and her images
as I dealt with Samaria and her idols?' "

When the Lord has finished all his work against Mount Zion and Jerusalem, he will say, "I will punish the king of Assyria for the willful pride of his heart and the haughty look in his eyes. For he says: "By the strength of my hand I have done this,

and by my wisdom, because I have understanding.
I removed the boundaries of nations,

I plundered their treasures;
like a mighty one I subdued their kings.

As one reaches into a nest,
so my hand reached for the wealth of the nations;
as men gather abandoned eggs,
so I gathered all the countries;
not one flapped a wing,
or opened its mouth to chirp. "

Think of Goliath.

Listen to him in these verses from I Samuel 17.

A champion named Goliath, who was from Gath, came out of the Philistine camp. He was over nine feet tall. He had a bronze helmet on his head and wore a coat of scale armor of bronze weighing five thousand shekels; on his legs he wore bronze greaves, and a bronze javelin was slung on his back. His spear shaft was like a weaver's rod, and its iron point weighed six hundred shekels. His shield bearer went ahead of him.

Goliath stood and shouted to the ranks of Israel, "Why do you come out and line up for battle? Am I not a Philistine, and are you not the servants of Saul? Choose a man and have him come down to me. If he is able to fight and kill me, we will become your subjects; but if I overcome him and kill him, you will become our subjects and serve us." Then the Philistine said, "This day I defy the ranks of Israel! Give me a man and let us fight each other." On hearing the Philistine's words, Saul and all the Israelites were dismayed and terrified...

Meanwhile, the Philistine, with his shield bearer in front of him, kept coming closer to David. He looked David over and saw that he was only a boy, ruddy and handsome, and he despised him. He said to David, "Am I a dog, that you come at me with sticks?" And the Philistine cursed David by his gods. "Come here," he said, "and I'll give your flesh to the birds of the air and the beasts of the field!"

3. The rest of us.

Most of the rest of us, as we grow up, learn to boast in ways that are not so flagrant or obvious. We boast subtly. As we become more aware of how foolish boasting can appear we learn to avoid doing it in glaring ways. But boasting is wrong even if it is subtle. Our mouth guards need to recognize when boasting is trying to slip by in subtle disguise.

Jesus' Mouth, the Image of God's Invisible Mouth

Jesus had everything to boast about. He was God! He was co-creator with His Father of the entire universe. He had all power. He was perfect, without sin. And yet, Jesus never let a word of boasting pass through his lips.

Jesus did not boast of His miracles, in fact he often asked others not to even mention them. Jesus did not boast about His works of kindness but did them quietly. Paul, in Philippians two instructs us to have the humility of Christ as we relate to one another.

> *In your relationships with one another, have the same mindset as Christ Jesus: Who, being in very nature God, did not consider equality with God something to be used to his own advantage rather, he made himself nothing by taking the very nature of a servant, being made in human likeness. And being found in appearance as a man, he humbled himself by becoming obedient to death— even death on a cross!*
> Philippians 2:5-8

May God enable us to imitate Christ by keeping boasting from our lips.

Lesson Eight
Review Questions

1. Define boasting.

2. Understanding three things should help us refrain from boasting. What are those three things?

Memorize:

May I never boast except in the cross of our Lord Jesus Christ, through which the world has been crucified to me, and I to the world.

Galatians 6:14

Lesson Nine
Detain Angry Words

My dear brothers, take note of this: Everyone should be quick to listen, slow to speak and slow to become angry, for man's anger does not bring about the righteous life that God desires.
James 1:19-20

The guards of our mouths should not let angry words pass.

Five Biblical Principles Regarding Angry Words:

1. Our mouths are not meant to be vents.

A fool gives vent to his anger,
but a wise man keeps himself under control.
Proverbs 29:11

Vent = "To relieve by means of a vent" or "To give vigorous or emotional expression to"

2. Angry words may be common, but they are a serious matter.

But I tell you that anyone who is angry with his brother will be subject to judgment. Again, anyone who says to his brother, 'Raca" is answerable to the Sanhedrin. But anyone who says, 'You fool" will be in danger of the fire of hell.
Matthew 5:22

3. Slowing down, listening to others, and thinking are a big part of the solution to the problem of angry words.

My dear brothers, take note of this: Everyone should be quick to listen, slow to speak and slow to become angry, for man's anger does not bring about the righteous life that God desires.
James 1:19-20

4. Don't let it marinate overnight.

In your anger do not sin. Do not let the sun go down while you are still angry.

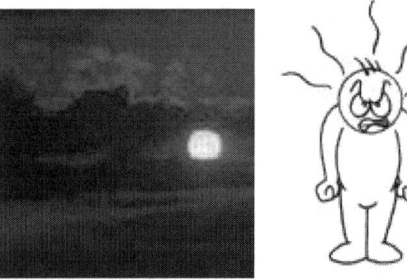

Ephesians 4:26

5. A quaint old hymn says, "Count your blessings name them one by one." Elizabeth Browning wrote in her poem, "How do I love thee, Let me count the ways." Kids like to count the pennies and dimes in their savings. **There are lots of good things to count, but someone's mistakes and sins are not one of them.**

No List Keeping

It (love) is not rude, it is not self seeking, it is not easily angered, it keeps no record of wrongs.
I Corinthians 13:5

If we catch an angry list of someone else's past sins flowing through our mouth, it's time to wake up the guard. Love keeps no record of wrongs.

> "A hundred times last year I had to tell you not to…."
>
> "Last month you…."
>
> "Last week you…."
>
> "Last night you … ***again***"
>
> "And now you have the nerve to …."

Jesus' Mouth, the Image of God's Invisible Mouth

Jesus, perfectly holy God, did express godly anger in His speech. But godly righteous anger is something that our anger very rarely is. Our anger is a selfish one that springs from being crossed or hurt. Our anger comes over us because we do keep a record of wrongs. In complete contrast with our lists of other people's wrongs, there is Jesus on the cross with a list of our wrong doings nailed beside Him. He not only refrains from listing them off to us, but he takes the list to the cross and dies for it.

"He forgave us all our sins, having canceled the written code, with its regulations, that was against us and that stood opposed to us, he took it away, nailing it to the cross."
Colossians 2: 13b-14

His loving sacrifice kept Him from angry words for us and it should keep us from angry words aimed at one another.

Lesson 9
Review Questions

List the five principles discussed above that have the potential to help you understand your anger and how to overcome it.

What is the difference between angry words Jesus spoke and the angry words we speak?

Memorize:

My dear brothers, take note of this: Everyone should be quick to listen, slow to speak and slow to become angry, for man's anger does not bring about the righteous life that God desires.
James 1:19-20

Lesson Ten
Seize Divisive Words
& Any that Tear Down

Divisive Words

Like earthly parents, one of the things dearest to the heart of God is the unity of His children. Jesus laid down his life to make us into one body.

The book of Ephesians describes God's yearning for our unity and the price he paid to provide for it.

For he himself is our peace, who has made the two one and has destroyed the barrier, the dividing wall of hostility, by abolishing in his flesh the law with its commandments and regulations. His purpose was to create in himself one new man out of the two, thus making peace, and in this one body to reconcile both of them to God through the cross, by which he put to death their hostility. He came and preached peace to you who were far away and peace to those who were near. For through him we both have access to the Father by one Spirit Consequently, you are no longer foreigners and aliens, but fellow citizens with God's people and members of God's household built on the foundation of the apostles and prophets, with Christ Jesus himself as the chief cornerstone. In him the whole building is joined together and rises to become a holy temple in the Lord. And in him you too are being built together to become a dwelling in which God lives by his Spirit. Ephesians 2:14-22

From him the whole body joined and held together by every supporting ligament, grows, and builds itself up in love, as each part does its work. Ephesians 4:16

Words that put walls up break the heart of God.

We need to guard against any words coming out of our mouths that will divide one person from another or ourselves from another. Unify. Do not divide. Scrutinize words before they exit your mouth. Ask, "Is this word going to build a partition or build the body? "

If *it is possible, as far as it depends on you, live at peace with everyone.* Romans 12:18

Six things the LORD hates; ... *A false witness who pours out lies, and a man who stirs up dissension among brothers.* Proverbs 6:16 - 19

God's alternative - The desire of God's heart:
How good and pleasant it is when brothers live together in unity! Psalms 133:1

Words that Tear Down

Some kids are very good at building block towers. Some toddlers are very persistent in knocking them over. SMASH! You recognize the scenario.

People use words like this too. Godly people have developed the art of using their words to build people up. You know when you are around them. You get built up. Others, toddler-like, only know how to tear people down.

The goal God sets for our speech is very clear:

Do not let any unwholesome talk come out of your mouths, **but only what is helpful for building others up according to their needs***, that it may benefit those who listen.* Ephesians 4:29

Set up a check point through which your words must pass. Instruct the guard of your mouth to verify.

- "Is this word going to benefit anyone?"
- "Will it bless?"
- "Will it encourage?"
- "Will it build someone up?"

If it doesn't pass the test, it does not pass through the lips.

Words that tear down = Opposite of words that build up.
Be sure your guard deters them.

If you keep on biting and devouring each other, watch out or you will be destroyed by each other.
Galatians 5:15

Jesus' Mouth, the Image of God's Invisible Mouth

One of the most profound passages in the New Testament in regard to Christ's earnest desire for unity among His followers is found in His prayer for us in John 17:20- 23

> *My prayer is not for them alone. I pray also for those who will believe in me through their message, that all of them may be one, Father, just as you are in me and I am in you. May they also be in us so that the world may believe that you have sent me. I have given them the glory that you gave me, that they may be one as we are one— I in them and you in me—so that they may be brought to complete unity. Then the world will know that you sent me and have loved them even as you have loved me.*

Jesus claims that His effectiveness, His reaching out to the world to bring us back to God is all tied up in our unity. The world will not recognize Him as God unless we are one. How could Christ ever have spoken a divisive word that would have torn us apart, and how can we, His followers, break His heart by doing so. He came to make us one. Let us not undo what He came to accomplish by speaking divisive words.

Lesson 10
Review Questions

Recognize divisive words and words that tear down.

Evaluate these words: Check one box.	It unites	It divides	It builds up	It tears down
Could you please get off the piano? Your playing always gives me such a headache!				
Wasn't that kind of Jane to give up her day to help Mary?				
What a neat idea!				
I can't believe she did that to you! That was so mean!				
Would you mind waiting until later to practice piano? I don't know why, but right now I have a really strange headache that is super sensitive to noise. I always enjoy your piano playing. I love cooking in the kitchen while you are playing. It makes the meal prep not seem like work to have the beautiful music to listen to.				
Do you like Mary? I used to, but I have noticed how she is **always** asking people for help lately and it makes me a little sick.				
That idea is not original to you is it? I didn't think you could come up with something that clever.				
You know, that **does seem** mean, but I bet there is some explanation for her behavior. I've never known her to do anything like that before. She has always been so kind. Remember that time she took all the kids to the doctors for the Jones? I remember thinking that I wished I was as thoughtful as she.				
Is THAT your highest test grade?				
I know Grace would love to have you join us. She misses you and is always asking how you're doing.				
Tom said your Sunday school lesson didn't get through to the kids at all. I think he's going to take his son out of your class.				

Memorize:

If it is possible, as far as it depends on you, live at peace with everyone.
Romans 12:18

*Do not let any unwholesome talk come out of your mouths, **but only what is helpful for building others up according to their needs**, that it may benefit those who listen.*
Ephesians 4:29

Lesson Eleven
Catch Curses and Protect the Lord's Name

*You shall not misuse the name of the LORD your God, for the LORD will not hold anyone
guiltless who misuses his name.*
Exodus 20:7

As we consider the topics of cursing and taking God's name in vain, we will find that, as
with all speech, the real issue is what is in our hearts. Our speech reflects what we believe
and who we are. Our understanding of God, and our love for him, are the determining
factors in our not taking his name in vain or cursing in other ways. Read on to see why.

There are at least two different meanings to the word "Curse".

1. One meaning of "curse" is to wish evil upon someone we are angry with. Unlike the
godly anger recorded in a few Psalms (see Psalm 109), anger aimed at the enemies of
God, our cursing is not pleasing and acceptable.

God tells us to return good for evil.

Matthew 5:44 *"But I tell you: Love your enemies and pray for those who persecute you,
that you may be sons of your Father in heaven. He causes his sun to rise on the evil and
the good, and sends rain on the righteous and the unrighteous."*

Matthew 5: 39 *"If someone strikes you on the right cheek, turn to him the other also."*

We are to bless and pray for those that curse us.

Luke 6:28 *"Bless those who curse you, pray for those who ill treat you."*

2. The other meaning of "curse" is to take something that is holy or precious and private
and speak of it as an evil ugly thing. To curse is to profane the holy. Cursing shocks by
taking something out of its proper God given context.

The most beautiful and holy thing of all of course, is God himself. God is holy. He is
perfect in every way. The most horrible and direct manner of cursing is to misuse the
name of God. God made this one of the Ten Commandments that teaches us about him.

When we know and love God and our goal is to benefit those who listen to us, cursing and all unwholesome talk become foolish and undesirable things. Because of who we are in Christ we want to use our mouths to bless others, not curse them.

The Third Commandment

Exodus 20:7 *"You shall not misuse the name of the LORD your God, for the LORD will not hold anyone guiltless who misuses his name."*

If we study the scriptures and walk with God, if we know him in all his glory, and if we make a study of the names God used for himself in the Bible, as they reveal his character to us, the thought of misusing his name, or taking it lightly, becomes more and more heinous to us. His name is precious and sacred to be revered and held high.

The apostle Paul reiterates the importance of the third commandment in both Ephesians 5:4 *"Nor should there be obscenity...,"* (speech that is indecent, abominable, disgusting, repulsive, offensive to morality – dragging God's name in the mud big time)

And in Ephesians 4:29 *"Do not let any unwholesome talk come out of your mouths, but only what is helpful for building others up according to their needs, that it may benefit those who listen."*

When we know and love God and our goal is to benefit those who listen to us, cursing and all unwholesome talk become foolish and undesirable things. Because of who we are in Christ we want to use our mouths to bless others, not curse them.

John Piper's Sermon on Ephesians 4:29.

John Piper in a sermon on Ephesians 4:29 has helpfully suggested that Paul has four types of speech in mind when he commands us not to let unwholesome talk come out of our mouths. He shows us that what is in our hearts regarding God will control what comes out of our mouths.

"Now what sort of talk does Paul have in mind when he says, "Let no rotten talk come out of your mouth"? Let me suggest at least four kinds of language that I think Paul would include as "rotten" or "decayed" or "spoiled".

PIPER'S FOUR TYPES OF UNWHOLESMOE TALK
1- Taking the Lord's Name in Vain

First would be language that takes the name of the Lord in vain. It is a great contradiction of who we are as Christians if we say, "God!" or "My God!" or "God Almighty!" or "Christ!" or "Jesus!" just because we are mad or surprised or amazed. No one with a good marriage would stomp on his wedding ring to express anger. It stands for something precious and pure. And so does the name of God and Jesus Christ.

2- Language that trivializes terrible realities

The second kind of language that Paul would call rotten would be language that trivializes terrible realities—like hell and damnation and holiness. What's wrong with saying, "What the hell!" or "Hell, no" or "Go to hell!" or "Damn it!" or "Damn right!" or "Holy cow!" or "Holy mackeral!"?

Among other things these expressions trivialize things of terrible seriousness. It's simply a contradiction to believe in the horrible reality of hell and use the word like a punctuation mark for emphasis when talking about sports or politics. The same is true of damnation. And if the divine command, "Be holy as I am holy," carries for you the same weight it carried for Moses and Jesus and the apostles, you will simply find that "Holy cow" or holy anything will stick in your throat because it treats something infinitely precious as a trifle.

3- Vulgar References to Sex and the Human Body

The third kind of language I think Paul would include in his command not to let any rotten talk come out of your mouth is vulgar references to sex and the human body. With this kind of language people take good things that God has made, and use them like mud to smear on whatever they get upset about. The whole assumption behind the use of vulgar four-letter words is that they communicate scorn or disdain or hate. How does this happen?

How, for example, does the act of sexual relations, created by God as good to be fulfilled in marriage—how does it get translated into a four letter word and carry the meaning of hate and scorn? The answer is easy: first you get God out of your mind. That's fundamental to all vulgarity. Then you get the sanctity of his creation out of your mind. And then, in your mind, you replace the tenderness of married love with the force of rape, and you've got yourself four letter word which does verbally the same thing that rape does physically: it expresses selfish, uncaring abusiveness. (Which, incidentally, is why I would say to Christian women, don't spend two minutes with a man who uses this kind of language: rape and rotten language come from exactly the same root.)

4- Mean-Spirited Language like "Shut up!"

The final kind of language I think Paul would call rotten is mean-spirited language—like, "Shut up!" The words themselves are untarnished. But the usage is vicious and loveless."

Jesus' Mouth, the Image of God's Invisible Mouth

When it comes to learning not to curse people, and to hold the name of God sacred, Christ is surely our perfect example. Far from cursing those who cause Him pain, we see Jesus, at the very point of lying down His life for us, crying out in pain both:

"My God, My God, why have you forsaken me?" Matthew 27:46
And
"Father, forgive them, for they do not know what they are doing." Luke 232:34

Lesson 11
Review Questions

What are the four types of unwholesome talk Piper believes Paul refers to in Ephesians 4:29?

"Do not let any unwholesome talk come out of your mouths, but only what is helpful for building others up according to their needs, that it may benefit those who listen."

1.

2.

3.

4.

We said above, "If we study the scriptures and walk with God, if we know him in all his glory, and if we make a study of the names God used for himself in the Bible, as they reveal his character to us, the thought of misusing his name, or taking it lightly, becomes more and more heinous to us. His name is precious and sacred to be revered and held high. "

What are some of the names of God he uses for himself in the scriptures?
(The answer to this is not in the lesson.)

Memorize:

You shall not misuse the name of the LORD your God, for the LORD will not hold anyone guiltless who misuses his name.
Exodus 20:7

Lesson Twelve
Jail Loud, Obnoxious, Disruptive, and Silly Words

Nor should there be obscenity, foolish talk or coarse joking, which are out of place, but rather thanksgiving.
Ephesians 5:4

Compared to major offenses such as lies, gossip, boasting, or destructive criticism which are all highlighted as fierce enemies to be guarded against, silly, obnoxious, or disruptive words might be called inconspicuous mini enemies.

However, the fact that they are less conspicuous makes us less wary of them and less apt to bother training the guards of our mouths to watch for them, resulting in the free flow of such things from our mouths. The outcome is that God is dishonored. It is very worthwhile to consider these words and note what the Bible has to say about them. We can't have a mouth like His if we do not guard against obnoxious, disruptive and silly words.

Silliness:
Ephesians 5:4 *"Nor should there be obscenity, foolish talk or coarse joking, which are out of place, but rather thanksgiving."*

Let's look first at "silly" words because fishing out the silly words from our conversations without becoming dour and sullen is a bit tricky.

C. S. Lewis' Puddleglum, with the emphasis on **glum,** is a character that takes life soberly. At first he seems only gloomy like Eeyore. But Puddlelglum is a true hero who wisely sees the seriousness of life and responds to it admirably. He is a funny entertaining mixture of extreme pessimism and marvelous faithfulness, loyalty, and determination who turns out a loveable and honorable character.

"They all say – I mean, the other wiggles all say- that I'm too flighty; don't take life seriously enough. If they've said it once, they've said it a thousand times. "Puddleglum," they've said, "You're altogether too full of bobance and bounce and high spirits. You've got to learn that life isn't all fricasseed frogs and eel pie. You want something to sober you down a bit..." The Silver Chair, C. S. Lewis

Does saying that believers should not be silly or tell coarse jokes mean that a sense of humor is a bad thing? Is laughter bad? Should believers be somber?

Look at what these three men of faith have to say about humor:

C. H. Spurgeon's Great Sense of Humor

Larry J. Michael, PhD, has written an article on the humor of Charles Spurgeon. *Charles Spurgeon's Humor* **which can be found at** **http://www.evangelicalpress.com/spurgeon/**

Listen to Michael's beautiful description of Spurgeon's sense of humor:

Spurgeon's great sense of humor

Many evangelicals know well the stern side of C. H. Spurgeon and his serious pursuit of the holy life. Indeed, his stands for righteous causes, and countering doctrinal error are often recounted. But many readers may not know that he was a man with a great sense of humor. Spurgeon knew the value of laughter and mirth. He virtually took to heart the word in Proverbs 17:22: "A merry heart doeth good like a medicine."

Spurgeon laughed as often as he could. He laughed at the ironies of life, he laughed at comical incidents, he laughed at the amusing elements of nature. He sometimes laughed at his critics. He loved to share wholesome jokes with his friends and colleagues in ministry. He was known to tell humorous stories from the pulpit. William Williams, a fellow pastor who kept company with Spurgeon, was a near and dear friend in the latter years of Spurgeon's life. He wrote:

> *What a bubbling fountain of humor Mr. Spurgeon had! I laughed more, I verily believe, when in his company than during all the rest of my life besides. He had the most fascinating gift of laughter ... and he had also the greatest ability for making all who heard him laugh with him. When someone blamed him for saying humorous things in his sermons, he said, "He would not blame me if he only knew how many of them I keep back."*

Spurgeon considered humor such an integral part of his ministry that a whole chapter in his autobiography is devoted to it. Humor permeates his sermons and writings, often woven into the fabric of his messages. It's one reason among many why he is still so readable today.

G. K. Chesterton's Great Sense of Humor

G. K. Chesterton once said, "a characteristic of the great saints is their power of levity. Angels can fly because they take themselves lightly."

Chesterton had an incredibly fun sense of humor that permeates all his writings and makes them rich and fun as well as being tremendously edifying.

Chesterton did not believe that God meant for our spirits to be always heavy and grave, living in total seriousness. Chesterton's pun about being light hearted is also well known, "Satan fell by the force of gravity." Chesterton would say that the devil took himself too seriously, too gravely. God does not want us to do that. Christ Jesus raises us out of heaviness into lightness when we quit taking ourselves seriously. Jesus is the light of the world and He makes the world lighter on our shoulders. He gives us the easy yoke, the light burden. He is bringing an end to gravity and the grave. He invites us to soar with the angels on the wings of holy laughter.

Piper's mother's Sense of Humor

John Piper once described his mother, "mingled with fiercely earnest faith in the realities in heaven and hell and the seriousness of the Christian life, my mother had an utterly uninhibited sense of humor. "

What about us? How do we balance avoiding course joking or silliness with having a wholesome sense of humor?

What does the Bible say? The Bible talks a lot about joy and a little about laughter. One verse that makes it clear that we have a lot to be joyful about and that our joy should overflow into laughter is

Psalm 126: 1-3 *"When the LORD brought back the captives to Zion, we were like men who dreamed. Our mouths were filled with laughter, our tongues with songs of joy. Then it was said among the nations, The LORD has done great things for them. The LORD had done great things for us, and we are filled with joy."*

We know that God does not disapprove of merriment.
"A cheerful **heart** is good medicine, but a crushed spirit dries up the bones." Proverbs 17:22

As believers we should have a sober understanding of who God is, who we are and what the needs around us are. While enjoying wholesome laughter and humor, we should not trivialize or defile God's creation. Being silly, lacking discretion, or course joking often come from not remembering the seriousness of life and the beauty of God's handiwork, or of not loving and discerning our neighbor's needs and sensitivities. We need to consider whether the words we are about to speak are wholesome and beneficial.

In Ephesians 5:4 *"Nor should there be obscenity, foolish talk or coarse joking, which are out of place, but rather thanksgiving."* thanksgiving is given as the antidote to obscenity, foolish talk, and coarse joking. Why? Because we are new creatures in Christ putting on the new man and we are now seeing creation and God's redemption more clearly for what it is and we are full of gratitude. Our view of these things in Christ fills us with gratitude not silliness. The balance we need is the balance of portraying things as they really are.

Obnoxious Words

Controlling obnoxious words or disruptive ones is not as tricky as controlling silly words, because there is no fear of losing something good in the process like the fear that accompanies the warning to "not be silly".

Proverbs 27:14 "*If a man loudly blesses his neighbor early in the morning, it will be taken as a curse.,* conveys just about all we need to know about obnoxious words. Avoiding them is a matter of being thoughtful and considerate.

Disruptive Words

Disruptive words are much the same way. Avoiding them comes from being aware of others around you, and taking thought for the right moment to speak.

"*But everything should be done in a fitting and orderly way.*"   I Corinthians 14:40

Jesus' Mouth, the Image of God's Invisible Mouth

Certainly Jesus never spoke an obnoxious word. Nor do we see Him being disruptive. He is quiet and patient and does not draw attention to himself at all.

The Bible provides very little information about Jesus' sense of humor. There are several different opinions regarding His sense of humor. Some people see humor in some of His parables. (A camel going through the eye of a needle) The arguments as to whether there is humor there are interesting and good on both sides but perhaps inconclusive.

We certainly see joy in Christ. He is certainly kind, gentle, friendly, thoughtful and full of love. And these are more important characteristics. We actually want them more and appreciate them more than we do humor- in anybody. Jesus was not dour, but he was very understandably called "a man of sorrows." His life was serious. It was one big sacrifice. He was a focused man. He had a purpose. If there is humor in any of his parables it is certainly humor born out of a purpose. It is hard to imagine Jesus studying to be funny and beefing up his humor or even hoping for a laugh from his listeners. Examining Christ's words points us more towards expression of a satisfied joy and delight than it does towards humor. You might want to read a book that deals with the subject of Jesus' humor and think more about this subject.

Lesson 12
Review Questions

Did Christ have a sense of humor? How did he use it?

How about the perfect example of Christ? What do you think? Did Jesus have a sense of humor? Did Jesus tell any jokes? This is an interesting question and it does help us towards a balance. Write down what you think about Jesus having a sense of humor and explain why.

How can the guards of our mouths recognize when our humor is displeasing to God? What kind of humor might please Him? What kind is wrong? Write up a clear description for the guard of your mouth to be trained by.

Obnoxious Words

Proverbs 27:14 "If a man loudly blesses his neighbor early in the morning, it will be taken as a curse."

How many analogous situations can you think of?

Disruptive Words

"But everything should be done in a fitting and orderly way." I Corinthians 14:40

What does this have to do with our mouths?

Memorize:

Nor should there be obscenity, foolish talk or coarse joking, which are out of place, but rather thanksgiving. Ephesians 5:4

Lesson Thirteen
Demolish Foolish Words

"A fool's mouth is his undoing, and his lips are a snare to his soul."
Proverbs 18:7

We want to train the guard of our mouths to restrain foolish words.

The Bible talks about at least two kinds of fools or foolish talk.

I. First, and most consistently and profoundly, a fool according to the Bible is someone who does not recognize or acknowledge God in the way he talks.

- Psalm 14:1
  *The **fool says** in his heart, "There is no God."*

- Psalm 53:1
  *The **fool says** in his heart, "There is no God."*

- Proverbs 28:26 *"He who trusts in himself is a fool."*

- Proverbs 15:2 *"The tongue of the wise commends knowledge, but the mouth of the fool gushes folly."*

- Ezekiel 13:3
  *Woe to the **fool**ish prophets who follow their own spirit and have seen nothing!*

- Proverbs 1**:7**
  The fear of the LORD is the beginning of knowledge, but fools despise wisdom and discipline.

- Psalm 74:18
  Remember how the enemy has mocked you, O LORD, how foolish people have reviled your name.

A fool in the Bible is not necessarily an uneducated, dim witted or stupid person. A fool may be well educated and have a keen mind. In fact he may have a PhD and be looked up to. In I Corinthians we learn that the wisdom of the world is foolish and true wisdom can seem like foolishness to the world. Apart from God's work in our hearts and minds we would not recognize wisdom for what it is. Wisdom and folly are turned completely around. A person is a fool if he has forsaken God and is relying on his own self sufficient intellectual powers.

So what does this have to do with us? If God has shown us the truth and reveled himself to us, by his grace, we are no longer the fools we are inclined to be. But we want to look out for the ways in which we are not thinking and speaking consistently with the knowledge we have of who God is and who we are in Christ, the times we are forgetting about him.

Our concern should not be so much to avoid speaking like a fool in the world's understanding of being a fool. We may well sound like a fool to the world when we are sharing the truth of the gospel.

We need not worry much about seeming like an ignoramus. Grandma's not really a fool because she thinks you should buy a mouse trap when you tell her you have a new mouse. It's not the end of the world if you get the words geography and geology mixed up one time or slip and say Thomas Jefferson freed the slaves. The foolish words we want to watch out for more earnestly are the words we speak when we are forgetting God and speaking as though He is not there, being all powerful, all wise, righteous, or perfectly loving.

Analyze these expressions and explain what makes them **_foolish_** words:

1. "Nobody is going to care if I snitch just one of these."

2. "Darn, nothing ever goes right for me!"

3. "I am SO bored."

4. "The only thing I care about is how much money this is going to bring in."

5. "I worked so blasted hard on this thing and nobody even noticed or cared! What's the point?"

Can you think of any statement that comes out of your mouth frequently that is a truly **_foolish_** thing to say?

II. Secondly, a fool in scripture is someone who glories in his own speech. He talks too much about anything he knows without discretion because he loves to show off his knowledge. This may be in part because he fits the broader definition of a fool as someone who does not acknowledge God, and therefore thinks too highly of himself, but it is a kind of folly we are all prone to, believer and unbeliever.

- Proverbs 12:23 *"A prudent man keeps his knowledge to himself, but the heart of fools blurts out folly."*

- Proverbs 18:2 *"A fool hath no delight in understanding, but only that his heart may reveal itself"*

- Proverbs 18:6 *"A fool's lips bring him strife, and his mouth invites a beating."*

- Proverbs 17:27, 28 *"A man of knowledge uses words with restraint, and a man of understanding is even tempered. Even a fool is thought wise if he keeps silent, and discerning if he holds his tongue."*

- Ecclesiastes 10:12, 13 *"Words from a wise man's mouth are gracious, but a fool is consumed by his own lips. At the beginning his words are folly; at the end they are wicked madness—and the fool multiplies words."*

A mouth that glorifies God is a mouth that is trained to restrain foolish words. We should not think so highly of ourselves that we have to make sure everyone hears everything we know. We should not blurt out volumes of words that are accomplishing nothing but airing our own opinions and displaying our bank of information.

We should remember that we are God's creatures, and He is our Maker, so much bigger and infinitely wiser and better informed of everything! We should also take Paul's advice and consider others around us better than ourselves and realize they too have knowledge, opinions, and information of all kinds. We will want to train the guards of our mouths not to let us carry on at length about all our favorite subjects when it is not benefiting those who listen but merely making us feel good.

Lesson 13
Review Questions

1. Give two definitions of a fool in the Bible.

2. If a fool is defined as someone who does not acknowledge God, give two examples of a foolish statement that should not come out of our mouths.

Memorize:

The tongue of the wise commends knowledge, but the mouth of the fool gushes folly

Proverbs 15:2

Lesson Fourteen:
Capture Complaining and Grumbling Words

"Do everything without complaining or arguing, so that you may become blameless and pure, children of God without fault in a crooked and depraved generation, in which you shine like stars in the universe."

Philippians 2:14-15

Whine or Shine

We have a unique opportunity to shine –

OR

We can whine instead.

The stars are one of God's amazing creations. They have left humans confounded and awestruck for many generations. They have inspired poetry, songs and paintings. What little child never heard *Twinkle Twinkle Little Star*? Scientists are unraveling many awesome mysteries about them. They have entertained and blessed star gazers for thousands of years.

Some people have had stars named after them and have found that a great honor. But we have a chance to "be a star" well at least to be called "star-like" by God, who, after all, made the stars and knows what they are like. We are all familiar with Matthew 5:16 "Let your light shine before men." We know we Christians are to be light in this dark world. Philippians 2 that talks about us as *children of God without fault in a crooked and depraved generation, in which you shine like stars in the universe.* Like stars! The verse is poignant.

The familiar phrase, *Do everything without arguing or complaining*, is also from Philippians. I memorized it in Sunday school as a little girl. And as a Mom I find it a good reminder for my kids sometimes. But until a few years ago I did not consciously realize that these phrases are in the same verse! They go together. They are linked. They are dependent. The verse says that we should do everything without arguing or complaining, SO THAT we can be shining stars in a dark crooked twisted needy world!

That gives us a choice. We can whine, or we can shine.

This world is hard and every one runs into difficulties and distressing times. Things do not always seem "fair". In a sense you can say there is a lot to complain about. So the world is full of complainers. Many people complain habitually, about everything. For unbelievers who do not understand that this is a fallen world and that there is hope in Christ, complaining makes some sense. They want to be treated fairly. They do not understand why things go badly. Things are dark and confusing. But as believers, we have no excuse to complain. We understand where all the evil came from. We know about God's loving plan and great sacrifice on our behalf to set things right. We have God's good promises. We know he will set everything right in the end. We know we have a bright hope in Christ. We know, because Romans 8:28 tells us so, that in the meanwhile, *"All things work together for good to those who love God and are called according to his purpose."* We are called to be thankful, not to complain. And when we really fulfill this calling of thankfulness instead of complaining, we do stand out. We are different. The world will look and see us shining. We will be pointing the way to God. We will glorify him by doing everything we do without arguing or complaining.

We must train the guards of our mouths to be on the lookout for grumbling or complaining. Why is this so important?

God's perspective on our complaints:

Think about it.

God made us.

He gives us everything we need.

He gives us MORE than we need. He provides things to enjoy.

He loves us sacrificially. When we rebelled and got ourselves lost and in deep trouble, he planned our redemption at terrific cost to Himself and carried it out.

He loves us with a perfect love.

His love is informed. He knows and understands and loves according to our true needs.

His love is tireless and patient.

And then, in return, we grumble, grumble, and grumble. We are terrible complainers.

How very painful that has to be to God. How deeply our complaints must hurt him.

God takes complaining very seriously:

God doesn't monkey around with complainers. Consider these verses.

- *"Now the people complained about their hardships in the hearing of the LORD, and when he heard them his anger was aroused. Then fire from the LORD burned among them and consumed some of the outskirts of the camp. 2 When the people cried out to Moses, he prayed to the LORD and the fire died down. 3 So that place was called Taberah, because fire from the LORD had burned among them.* Numbers 11:1-3

- *The LORD said to Moses and Aaron: "How long will this wicked community grumble against me? I have heard the complaints of these grumbling Israelites. So tell them, 'As surely as I live, declares the LORD, I will do to you the very things I heard you say: In this desert your bodies will fall—every one of you twenty years old or more who was counted in the census and who has grumbled against me. Not one of you will enter the land I swore with uplifted hand to make your home, except Caleb son of Jephunneh and Joshua son of Nun. As for your children that you said would be taken as plunder, I will bring them in to enjoy the land you have rejected. But you—your bodies will fall in this desert. Your children will be shepherds here for forty years, suffering for your unfaithfulness, until the last of your bodies lies in the desert. For forty years—one year for each of the forty days you explored the land—you will suffer for your sins and know what it is like to have me against you. I, the LORD, have spoken, and I will surely do these things to this whole wicked community, which has banded together against me. They will meet their end in this desert; here they will die."* Numbers 14:26-38

- *"And do not grumble, as some of them did—and were killed by the destroying angel.* I Corinthians 10:10

Are we ever allowed to complain?

Complaining and arguing are so common. They are the norm. Everyone complains about just about everything. This verse in Philippians tells us DO <u>EVERYTHING WITHOUT</u> COMPLAINING. We should not complain. Period. We are to trust. We are to be patient. We are to be thankful. Complaining is wrong.

Stop complaining about your job!

Does that mean there is no such thing as an appropriate complaint?

Actually there is a kind of complaint that could be called a Biblically warranted complaint, a complaint that God would call appropriate. (But most of our complaints do not fit this definition.)

Acts 6:1 tells us that, "In those days when the number of disciples was increasing, the Grecian Jews among them complained against the Hebraic Jews because their widows were being overlooked in the daily distribution of food." The Grecian Jews did what? They "complained."

Now at this time in the church things were quite in tense. In the previous chapter in Acts Annanias and his wife Sapphira lie about the price of a piece of land they sold and they are struck dead on the spot. So one might stand back and say, "Ok. What is going to happen to these Grecian Jews who are complaining? Look out."

But Peter and the rest of the Apostles don't correct these people for complaining. Instead they say, "You're right." And they appoint seven congregationally chosen men to oversee the distribution of food and make sure that all the widows are being treated fairly. They fixed the problem that was being complained about.

So we conclude that there's a kind of complaining that's appropriate, and there's a kind of complaining that's inappropriate.

There are two things that make up an acceptable legitimate complaint.

1. A complaint is acceptable if it is really about a legitimate issue. It must be a complaint about something that it is very important to change. A widow starving to death is something to be concerned about. We should see that it is dealt with. The specific color of the carpet in the new church building is not near and dear to the heart of God.

2. Acceptable complaints are legitimately raised when they are raised with people who have both the responsibility to do something about the situation and the ability to effect change in the situation. We can "shine like stars in the universe": if instead of complaining along with everyone else about the dorm food, we write a kind letter to the proper people in the administration, or if instead of complaining to everyone in the church about the pastor's four hour long sermons, we respectfully take our complaint to the pastor.

We want to train the guards of our mouths to realize that most of our complaints are not legitimate complaints. They should not come out of our mouths. They will keep us from being the bright shining stars in this dark universe that God calls us to be. We want to shine, not whine!

Jesus' Mouth, the Image of God's Invisible Mouth

We whine and whimper in the face of the tiniest injustice we experience. Jesus who never sinned at all, but was absolutely perfect in every way, suffered utterly "unfairly." He did not deserve the wrath of God as we all do. The mocking, the whipping, the crown of thorns, and His cruel suffering and death on the cross were utterly undeserved. But He never opened His mouth in complaint.

Meditate on Isaiah's description of our suffering Savior and His lack of complaint will astound you.

Isaiah 53: 3-7

> *He was despised and rejected by men, a man of sorrows and familiar with suffering. Like one from whom men hide their faces he was despised and we esteemed him not. Surely he took up our infirmities and carried our sorrows yet we considered Him stricken by God .smitten by Him and afflicted. But He was pierced for our transgressions. He was crushed by our iniquities. The punishment that brought us peace was upon Him and by His wounds we are healed.*
> *We all like sheep have gone astray, each of us had turned to his own way, and the LORD had laid on Him the iniquity of us all. He was oppressed and afflicted yet He did not open His mouth. He was led like a lamb to the slaughter and as a sheep before her shearers is silent, so He did not open His mouth.*

Lesson 14
Review Questions

1. Why is it particularly heinous for a Christian to complain?

2. How seriously does God take grumbling? How do you know this?

3. What are the two critical factors of a legitimate complaint?

4. Under what condition do we shine like stars?

Memorize:

Do everything without complaining or arguing, so that you may become blameless and pure, children of God without fault in a crooked and depraved generation, in which you shine like stars in the universe.

Philippians 2:14-15

Lesson Fifteen:
Take Critical Words into Custody

A man who lacks judgment derides his neighbor, but a man of understanding holds his tongue.
Proverbs 11:12

I'm on guard against lies, reckless words, gossip, boasting, angry words, divisive words, curse words, taking the Lord's name in vain, obnoxious and silly words, foolish words, and complaints. What's next? Are there other words I should be on the lookout for?

Here is our next goal.

We must train the guard of our mouths to stop criticism before it exits the door of our mouths because we know judgment is not our job. It's something God is far far better at than us and he plans to take care of it!

Romans 14:10-13

Why do you pass judgment on your brother? Or you, why do you despise your brother? For we will all stand before the judgment seat of God; for it is written, "As I live, says the Lord, every knee shall bow to me, and every tongue shall confess to God." So then each of us will give an account of himself to God. Therefore let us not pass judgment on one another any longer, but rather decide never to put a stumbling block or hindrance in the way of a brother.

What God desires of us is not keeping each other in place or putting each other down with constant criticism. On the contrary, what he calls us to is quite the opposite.

As a prisoner for the Lord, then, I urge you to live a life worthy of the calling you have received. Be completely humble and gentle; be patient, bearing with one another in love. Make every effort to keep the unity of the Spirit through the bond of peace.
Ephesians 4:1-3.

Unity is what God cares about, and establishing unity rules out criticizing each other.

What makes us critical of others?

i)   When we are hurt we retaliate with criticism.

ii)   Sometimes we feel hurt because no one noticed the good work we did.

iii)   Other times we retaliate with criticism when someone meanly criticizes us or misjudges us and harms our reputation.

It's amazing how when someone is nice to us and we feel close to them we are very unlikely to criticize them for anything they do. We forgive and forbear readily. But when someone has been mean to us and hurt us, we see their faults so vividly and we feel we just cannot tolerate them. We have to bring them up and talk about them. We feel justified in criticizing them.

How can we stop criticism at the door of our mouths?

1. If we are feeling critical of others because they have not given us credit or thanked us for our hard work we can stop the criticism by remembering that God is the one we most want to please. We keep him in mind.

   Jesus said in Matthew 6:4, 6, 18 *"Your Father who sees in secret will reward you."* We recall that we care more about what he thinks of us than anyone else. He sees. He knows. He even keeps records of what we do. We do what we do to please him, not others. The reward of his pleasure is much greater than any other notice! We can talk to him and ask him to help us not feel sorry for ourselves and to keep on doing good just for him. We ask him to help us not feel critical of others. Perhaps we are not aware of all the hard work they are doing either. We trust God and leave judgment to him.

2. If we are tempted to criticize someone because they have criticized us cruelly or unjustly, again, we remember God.

   Paul tells us in Romans 12:19-20, *"Beloved do not avenge yourselves, but give place to wrath. For it is written, 'Vengeance is mine, I will repay, says the Lord.' No, 'if your enemy is hungry, feed him; if he is thirsty, give him drink.'"*

   We should not criticize because we have been criticized.

Constructive Criticism

Sometimes (a minute percentage of the time) we speak critical words to be constructive because we are genuinely concerned for others, for God's glory, and the furtherance of His kingdom in a pure and disinterested way

If we are contemplating a critical word for the sake of God's glory and kingdom we should proceed with the utmost caution. Our hearts are so deceptive.

It is very rare that we are pure and disinterested. We should examine ourselves carefully and see if there is another motive involved. Are we sure we are not just trying to put someone else in their place?

This is not to say there is no place for constructive criticism. Just as we defined the proper appropriate instance of complaining, there is an appropriate kind of criticism; a gentle, loving, wise, Biblically founded, and well-prayed-over exhortation of someone we are truly loathe to hurt or offend. We will look at this kind of constructive criticism under "exhortation" in PART III of A Mouth Like His.

But we should rarely conclude that it is our job to set people right with criticism. Why?

Because we "have logs" in our own eyes.

> *"Do not judge, or you too will be judged. For in the same way you judge others, you will be judged, and with the measure you use, it will be measured to you.*
>
> *"Why do you look at the speck of sawdust in your brother's eye and pay no attention to the plank in your own eye? How can you say to your brother, 'Let me take the speck out of your eye,' when all the time there is a plank in your own eye? You hypocrite, first take the plank out of your own eye, and then you will see clearly to remove the speck from your brother's eye."*
>
> Matthew 7:1-5

We are ill suited to the task because we are so often blind to our own foolishness and sinfulness. We are quite capable of criticizing others for something we do ourselves.

2. **EVEN if we _were_ perfect** we should <u>still</u> be very reluctant to resort to criticism. Jesus himself, who was perfect, did not take on the job. He leaves it to the Father.

John 12:47

"As for the person who hears my words but does not keep them, I do not judge him. For I did not come to judge the world, but to save it."

Jesus says, *"When he looks at me, he sees the one who sent me. I have come into the world as a light..."* He showed by his life what God wants of us and who God is. If this is the attitude of Christ, it should be ours too. We show the way not by constantly harping on it and correcting everyone with our verbal lashes, whipping them into a better path, but by *living* the way and leaving the judgment to God the Father.

Jesus' Mouth, the Image of God's Invisible Mouth

The example of Christ is beautiful. We are to be like him. We don't try to make sure people who have put us down get put down too. Listen to what Jesus is like as described in 1 Peter 2:18-25

Servants, be submissive to your masters with all respect, not only to the kind and gentle but also to the overbearing. For one is approved if, mindful of God, he endures pain while suffering unjustly. For what credit is it, if when you do wrong and are beaten for it *you take it patiently? But if when you do right and suffer for it you take it patiently, you have God's approval. For to this you have been called, because Christ also suffered for you, leaving you an example, that you should follow in his steps. **He committed no sin; no guile was found on his lips. When he was reviled, he did not revile in return; when he suffered, he did not threaten; but he trusted to him who judges justly.** He himself bore our sins in his body on the tree, that we might die to sin and live to righteousness. By his wounds you have been healed. For you were straying like sheep, but have now returned to the Shepherd and Guardian of your souls.*

Jesus "trusted to him who judges justly."

This is what we need to do.

Want to stop being critical? Like Jesus, learn to trust God to do the judging and there will be "no guile found on your lips".

Lesson 15
Review Questions

1. What usually inspires people to speak critical words?

2. We can stop critical words by remembering things.

A. If we are feeling critical of others because they have not given us credit or thanked us for our hard work what should we recall and meditate on?

B. If our critical thoughts are inspired by being cruelly or unjustly criticized ourselves what should our thought process be to clear away the critical feelings?

3.   The amazing example of Jesus

Jesus is the only perfectly perfect person who ever lived. His temptation to criticize must have been so much greater than ours because there was nothing in him to criticize. Yet he never resorted to sinful impatient angry criticism. When he was treated unjustly, as he was to a infinitely greater extent than we will ever be, he did not retaliate with criticism. According to I Peter 2, how did Jesus do this? What did he meditate on?

Memorize:

A man who lacks judgment derides his neighbor, but a man of understanding holds his tongue.
Proverbs 11:12

Lesson Sixteen:
Confiscate "Too-Many-Words"

When words are many, sin is not absent, but he who holds his tongue is wise.
Proverbs 10:19

Sometimes there is nothing particularly sinful about the words coming out of our mouths, and yet the guard at the gate of our lips still needs to be watchful. If we speak many words Proverbs tells us that sin will show up. We are frequently inclined to use too many words. We like the sound of our own voices. We feel important if we are center stage. The Bible warns us of the dangers and disadvantages of too many words.

- The more the words, the less the meaning, and how does that profit anyone?
Ecclesiastes 6:11

- But I tell you that men will have to give account on the Day of Judgment for every careless word they have spoken.
Matthew 12:36

A POWERFUL CONTRAST

The book of Ecclesiastes provides us with a powerful contrast. We can spout off and babble on, thinking highly of our many words and our great ideas

OR
We can stand in awe of God!

Much dreaming and many words are meaningless. Therefore stand in awe of God.
Ecclesiastes 5:7

Jesus' Mouth, the Image of God's Invisible Mouth

Make a study of the four gospels and notice how few words Jesus uses. Often times when we would have much to say, He is completely silent. Sometimes He is presented with a complex question that most of us would spend days discussing and then days presenting our response to and Jesus manages to give a wise, helpful, true response in just a sentence. Jesus was not a man of many words. His well-chosen words were packed with meaning and wisdom.

Lesson 16
Review Questions

1. Spend an hour this week being alone and quiet. Meditate on these verses about too many words.

2. Sometime during this week choose a few hours during which you listen extra thoughtfully and carefully to others, practice being aware of the presence of God, and, as much as possible without being rude, keep your thoughts, ideas, and comments to yourself. (This should be a time during which you are interacting with others and would normally chatter some.) Did you experience the value of *not-too-many-words*? This is good practice for finding a better balance in everyday life.

Memorize:

When words are many, sin is not absent, but he who holds his tongue is wise.
Proverbs 10:19

Part II: A Well Trained Guard
Mouth Guard Boot Camp Exam

List the "Word Enemies" that God has told
us in His Word to guard against.

1. _____

2. _____

3. _____

4. _____

5. _____

6. _____

7. _____

8. _____

9. _____

10. _____

11. _____

12. _____

Recite all the Part II Bible Memory Verses

Psalm 33:6	
Isaiah 55:11, Isaiah 40:8	
James 3:4-5, Proverbs 18:21	
Psalms 141:3, Proverbs 30:5	
Proverbs 12:22	
Proverbs 12:18	
Proverbs 11:13	
Galatians 6:14	
James 1: 19-20	
Romans 12:18, Ephesians 4:29	
Exodus 20:7	
Ephesians 5:4	
Proverbs 15:2	
Philippians 2: 14-15	
Proverbs 11:12	
Proverbs 10:19	

At the close of PART II
Remember David and Trust in Jesus.

David sensed the value of the unique gift of thought and speech that is ours as image bearers of God. He grasped the beauty and magnificence of God's life- giving, life-sustaining, flawless mouth. He wrote in Psalm 33, "*By the word of the Lord were the heavens made, their starry host by the breath of his mouth.*" He realized his own mouth was meant to be a reflection, and he knew God had suggested setting a guard over his fallen mouth. *He who guards his mouth and his tongue keeps himself from calamity.*

David also knew that he was an utter failure at guarding his tongue. He cried out to God for help. *"Set a guard over my mouth, O, Lord, keep watch over my lips."* God's ultimate help for David, and for us, came in the form of Jesus. Only Jesus had a flawless mouth like His Father's. Jesus demonstrated the way to use a mouth, and he died to cover the damage we cause with our mouths every day. Outside Christ, none of us have any hope of doing the things we studied thus far. But, in Him, our mouths are reckoned perfect even now, even as we train the guard of our mouths. Keep reading Parts III and IV to see how God accomplishes the extraordinary redemption of our mouths.

PART III
A Fountain of Life

"The mouth of the righteous is a fountain of life."
Proverbs 10:11

Part III: A Fountain of Life

Introduction

Having graduated from our Mouth Guard Boot Camp we have a pretty clear idea what should **not** be allowed to pass out of our mouths. Now we turn our attention to what God does want us to use our mouths for.

God intends us to use our mouths the same way He uses His mouth. Our mouths are made in the likeness of His. In Christ we want to be renewed in the knowledge of our Creator and use our mouths the way He uses His.

Recall that God's mouth brings forth life. He spoke all living things into existence. We also see in verses like Deuteronomy 8:3 that the mouth of God is not only life giving, but life sustaining. His mouth gave us life, and our lives are sustained by his words.

He humbled you, causing you to hunger and then feeding you with manna, which neither you nor your fathers had known, to teach you that man does not live on bread alone but on every word that comes from the mouth of the LORD.   Deuteronomy 8:3

Our mouths are to become like his. We are to reflect his words. It is very interesting then, that in Proverbs God describes the mouth of the righteous as a fountain of life.

"The mouth of the righteous is a fountain of life ..."
Proverbs 10:11

Just like His mouth ours are meant to bring life and to nourish. **His mouth is the awesome, original, powerful fountain of life and ours are little reflections of His great and glorious mouth.**

The lips of the righteous nourish many… Proverbs 10:21

In Part III of A MOUTH LIKE HIS we will study how to imitate God's mouth. The glory and wonder of having mouths like His involves far more than learning what to avoid. So often that is all we emphasize. Training the guards of our mouths is necessary, but it is far from all we need to consider. We need to consider the reason He created us speaking beings. Let's move on now to contemplate the kinds of words that God yearns for us to speak, words that make our mouths into fountains of life! What a wonderful way to live and speak, bringing life to all around us!

WHAT KIND OF WORDS MAKE MY MOUTH A FOUNTAIN OF LIFE?

1. His Words -- Repeating after Him
2. Words of Praise
3. Words of Thanksgiving
4. Words that Instruct
5. Words that Heal
6. Words of Encouragement
7. Words that Comfort
8. Words of Counsel
9. Words of Exhortation
10. Words that Bring Smiles
11. Words that Testify and Share the Good News
12. Words of Confession

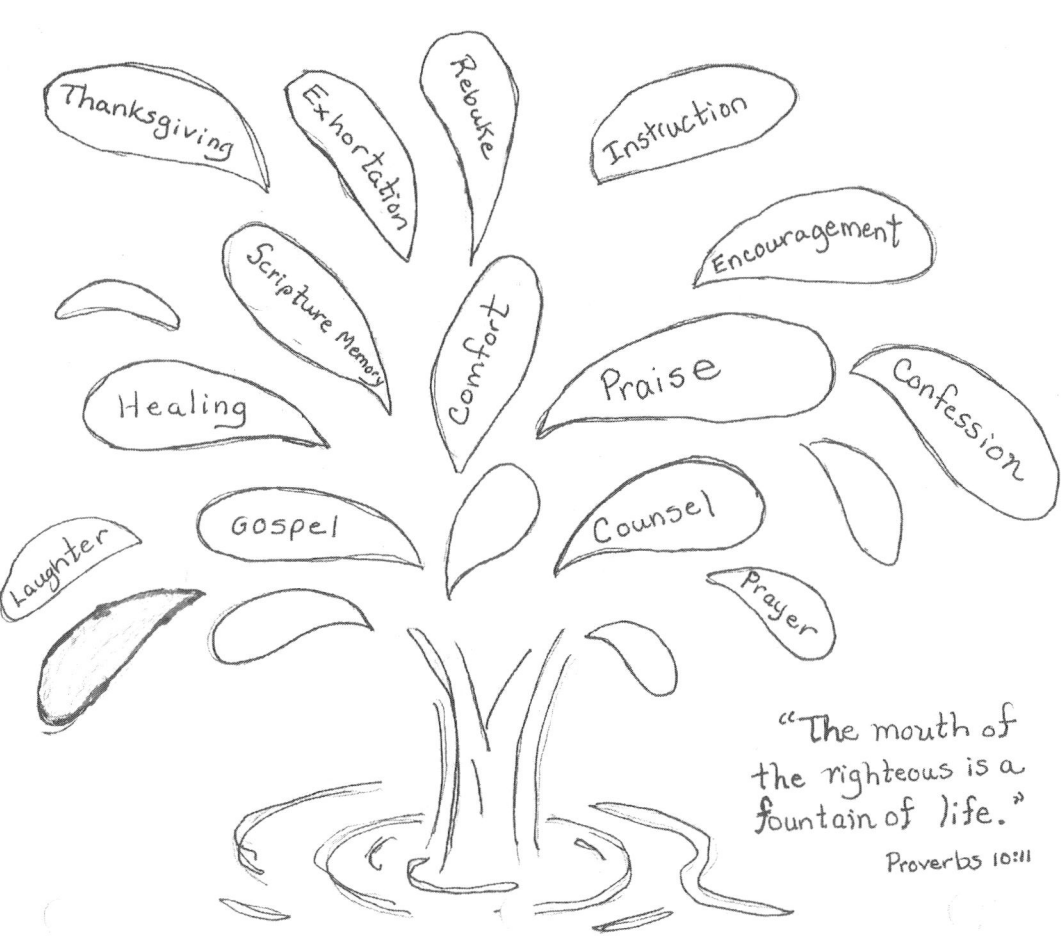

"The mouth of the righteous is a fountain of life."

Proverbs 10:11

Lesson Seventeen
Floods of Repetition

Do not let this Book of the law depart from your mouth
Joshua 1:8

If we want our mouth to reflect His mouth, to be a fountain of life like His, what better way than to practice by reciting His words?

Think about this. Have you ever studied a language that was foreign to you? What did you have to do? You listened and you repeated. Over and over you repeated. Maybe you have never learned a foreign language. But you did learn to speak your mother's language. As a toddler learns to speak by repeating over and over what he hears his parents saying, so we can learn the language of a life giving mouth by constant repetition of our Father's words.

Rehearsing His words over and over again will give our mouth great practice in our Father's tongue. We are rehearsing His words when we memorize and meditate on God's word. Repeating after Him, the maker of our mouth, is the best way to learn His language as well as the very best use of our mouth.

God has told us to do this in numerous places in Scripture.

- *"Do not let this Book of the law depart from your mouth; meditate on it day and night, so that you may be careful to do everything written in it. "*Joshua 1:8

- *I have hidden your word in my heart that I might not sin against you.   Praise be to you, O LORD; teach me your decrees.   **With my lips I recount all the laws** **that come from your mouth.*** Psalms 119:11-13

And, Christ has set the example for us in it.

Jesus' Mouth, the Image of God's Invisible Mouth

Jesus' mouth was frequently repeating His father's words. He often quoted Old Testament scriptures. They were in His mouth all the time. When Satan attacks Christ and tempts Him, Jesus' answers are pure Scripture. He set the example for us speaking His Father's words. Read through the gospels and note   Jesus' many quotations of Scripture.

The flawless mouth of Christ was frequently quoting God's Word. Our first step in making our mouths fountains of life like His is to constantly memorize, meditate on, and recite the Word of God.

Learn to speak your Father's language. Repeat it after Him.

Lesson 17
Review Questions

What is one absolutely necessary part of learning any tongue?

What is the most obvious and forth right way to learn to have a mouth like God's?

Find four examples of Jesus repeating His Father's Words.

Choose a chapter or a short passage from your Bible to commit to memory. Begin learning it today.

Keep on memorizing Scripture. Repeat His Words. Learn to speak in His tongue.

Memorize:

Do not let this Book of the law depart from your mouth
Joshua 1:8

Lesson Eighteen:

Gush with Praise

O Lord, open my lips, and my mouth will declare your praise.
Psalms 51:15

Our mouths were certainly made for praising their Maker.

- *My mouth will speak in praise of the LORD. Let every creature praise his holy name forever and ever.* Psalms 145:21

- *Let everything that has breath praise the LORD. Praise the LORD.* Psalms 150:6

- *From the lips of children and infants you have ordained praise because of your enemies, to silence the foe and the avenger.* Psalms 8:2

- *Great is the LORD and most worthy of praise; his greatness no-one can fathom.* Psalms 145:3

Our mouths were made to sing His praises.

- *Praise the LORD. How good it is to sing praises to our God, how pleasant and fitting to praise him!* Psalms 147:1

- *Sing to the LORD, you saints of his; praise his holy name.* Psalms 30:4

- *Sing the glory of his name; make his praise glorious!* Psalms 66:2

Two Categories of Praise:

We should develop a regular habit of praising God in our everyday lives, not just on special occasions or on Sunday. Our mouths should be characterized by praise. Psalm 150:2 suggests two categories of praise. Praise should come to mind both for who God is, and for what He has done. Speaking praise makes our mouths a fountain of life!

Praise him <u>for his acts</u> of power; praise him <u>for his surpassing greatness</u>.
Psalms 150:2

1. **Praise God for who he is. Praise Him for being:**

Holy	Kind	All powerful
Just	Righteous	Infinite & Eternal
Loving	Wise	Good
Pure	All knowing	Faithful

99

- *Let the name of the LORD be praised, both now and for evermore.* Psalms 113:2

- *My mouth is filled with your praise, declaring your splendor all day long.* Psalms 71:8

- *The LORD is my strength and my song; he has become my salvation. He is my God, and I will praise him, my father's God, and I will exalt him.* Exodus 15:2

2. **Praise God for what He has done and is doing.**

   - ♣ He created an awesome world and all the specifics in it
   - ♣ He redeemed us (and all of creation) through Christ
   - ♣ He takes providential loving care over us all the time
   - ♣ He disciplines us, guides us, and directs us

- *My mouth will tell of your righteousness, of your salvation all day long, though I know not its measure.* Psalm 11:35

- *I praise you because I am fearfully and wonderfully made; your works are wonderful, I know that full well.* Psalms 139:14

- *The centurion, seeing what had happened, praised God and said, "Surely this was a righteous man."* Luke 23:47

- *When he came near the place where the road goes down the Mount of Olives, the whole crowd of disciples began joyfully to praise God in loud voices for all the miracles they had seen:* Luke 19:37

Make it a habit to use your mouth for praise. It will bring life to those who hear you.

Jesus' Mouth, the Image of God's Invisible Mouth

Psalm 22: 22 is a Messianic verse describing Christ whose entire life was praise, His every thought, His every deed , His every word brought praise to the Father!

> *I will declare your name to my people;*
> *in the assembly I will praise you.*

Lesson 18
Review Questions

1. What are the two categories of praise suggested by Psalm 150:2?

2. Make a written list of five specific items of praise in each of these two categories. Go somewhere quiet and take the time to praise Him aloud. Practice the sound of praise coming from your mouth.

3. Cultivate the habit of praising God. If you think it would be helpful, choose a few set times or circumstances in which you can exercise this habit. Write down your commitments here, so you can review them.

   Examples:
   - Every morning before getting out of bed, praise God for something about His character.
   - Every day at lunch, give praise to God in front of others for one thing He has done that morning.
   - Start every prayer with praise for three of God's attributes.

Design your own commitment to practice praise that suits your life right now. Write it here.

Memorize:

My mouth is filled with your praise, declaring your splendor all day long.
Psalms 71:8

Lesson Nineteen:

Overflow with Thanksgiving

"Let us come before him with thanksgiving" Psalms 95:2

Giving thanks is another means of making our mouths a fountain of life.

We should thank God for our salvation.

- *Save us, O LORD our God, and gather us from the nations, that we may **give thanks** to your holy name and glory in your praise.* Psalm 106:47

- *But **thanks** be to God! He **gives** us the victory through our Lord Jesus Christ.* I Corinthians 15:57

We should thank God for good things, for answers to our cries for help, and for provisions we have received from Him.

- *I will **give** you **thanks**, for you answered me; you have become my salvation.* Psalm 118:21

- *Let them **give thanks** to the LORD for his unfailing love and his wonderful deeds for men."* A refrain from Psalm 107.

We should thank God all the time, for everything, under all circumstances.

We do not just thank Him when we feel like it or only for things that seem good to us. We recognize that God is wiser than we and that all things are from His hand. What he brings to us is good even if we are too small or foolish to see it at the time. Therefore we give thanks for everything.

- *Give thanks in all circumstances, for this is God's will for you in Christ Jesus.* 1 Thessalonians 5:18

- *...always giving thanks to God the Father for everything, in the name of our Lord Jesus Christ* Ephesians 5:20

There are two obvious reasons to give thanks. First, God commands us to. Second God deserves abundant expressions of our deep true gratitude more than we can ever fathom.

Give thanks to the LORD, for he is good. His love endures forever.
Psalms 136:1

Amazing Grace
Only God would do this.

We can and should give thanks because we are commanded to, and because it is profoundly sensible. But God, loving beyond comprehension, graciously turns even our thanksgiving around into a blessing on us!

There are at least three very significant benefits of expressing our thanks to God that are mentioned in Scripture. These three benefits come from my notes on a sermon preached by John Piper to whom I am greatly indebted and very grateful!

1. The first benefit of giving thanks is made clear in Romans 1:21.
Gratitude guards our souls and keeps us in right relationship with God. If we have seen how great God is and how marvelous his works are, but do not feel gratitude or express our thanks, our minds will be darkened. Lack of gratitude closes our minds to the truth of who God is and leaves us senseless and in the dark. Expressing thanks keeps us in the right relationship with the reality of who God is. It is a spiritually healthy response.

Although they knew God they did not glorify him as God or give thanks to him, but they became futile in their thinking and their senseless minds were darkened. Romans 1:21

2. A second benefit of giving thanks is made clear in Ephesians 5:4.
Thankfulness is a blessing in our relationships with other people. It helps us to interact in the right way. Giving thanks is a means of guarding against a vulgar and frivolous mouth. If we do not want to speak to others with resentment, complaining, filthiness, disrespect or ridicule, we can guard against these things by giving thanks instead. We can tell someone how thankful we are for them. We can thank them and we can thank God. To avoid being flippant, trivial, or silly we can fill our mouth with thanksgiving instead and thus become a fountain of life.

Try this. Give thanks, and see how refreshing it is.

Let there be no filthiness, nor silly talk, nor levity, which are not fitting; but instead let there be thanksgiving. Ephesians 5:4.

3. Finally, Philippians 4:6-7 states that thankfulness brings peace of mind.
This is a wonderful thing. God so designed our hearts and minds that when we focus on gratitude, when we notice His goodness and faithfulness, and express our thanks to Him, it has a way of settling our anxieties and quieting our concerns.

In everything by prayer and supplication with thanksgiving let your requests be made known to God. And the peace of God, which passes all understanding, will GUARD your hearts and minds in Christ Jesus. Philippians 4:6-7

God, who so lavishly deserves our thanks, kindly transforms thanksgiving into a blessing that returns to us. We should use our mouths for this holy and good purpose. Give thanks. Let your mouth be a fountain of life.

Jesus' Mouth, the Image of God's Invisible Mouth

Want to have a mouth like His? Compare your tongue with Christ's tongue. Consider how you give thanks and how He did. Sometimes we remember to thank God after He has dramatically answered our prayers. We regularly chant grace over a meal giving a nod of thanks for God's provisions. But Christ lived a life of giving thanks. He gave thanks for simple things in all kinds of circumstances. The four gospels do not overwhelm us with numerous examples of Jesus giving thanks, but we see enough to realize that He surrounded every type of moment with thankfulness. We see enough to realize that giving thanks was a way of life to Jesus.

In John chapter eleven we see Jesus standing before the cave that held the dead body of His dear friend Lazarus. What was he doing? Giving thanks.

In John chapter six we see Jesus surrounded and overwhelmed by a huge crowd of people full of loneliness, sorrow, sickness, and brokenness. He had been teaching and healing for hours. He sees their exhaustion, (heedless of His own) and their hunger (heedless of His own) and He realizes there are no Wal-Marts and no Panera Breads, no inns, or roadside farm stands. He is facing thousands of hungry people and all their needs and what is He doing? Giving thanks.

Near the end of His life Jesus sat around a table with His disciples. He was filled with sorrow and grief. He was flooded with thoughts and concerns for His disciples. He was overwhelmed with what He faced. He knew He was about to be nailed to a cross. He knew He was about to experience a separation from His Father that He had never known from all eternity. There before those He loved and cared for in this most intense situation, what is He doing even as He instructs them about the deepest thing ever? Giving thanks.

And when he had given thanks, he broke it and said, "This is my body, which is for you; do this in remembrance of me."
I Corinthians 11:24

May our mouths become like His expressing thanks to the Father in every situation.

Lesson 19
Review Questions

1. What two simple obvious reasons are there for giving thanks to God?

2. List three ways in which giving thanks ends up blessing us.

3. How often do you thank God during the day? Thank Him right now.

Memorize:

Let us come before him with thanksgiving.
Psalms 95:2

Although they knew God they did not glorify him as God or give thanks to him, but they became futile in their thinking and their senseless minds were darkened.
Romans 1:21

Lesson Twenty:

Spew Forth Godly Instruction

The teaching of the wise is a fountain of life, turning a man from the snares of death.
Proverbs 13:14

It's gloriously apparent. Teaching the truth is a way to have a mouth like God's. Proverbs communicates clearly that the mouth of a wise teacher is a fountain of life like His.

Teaching truth turns people away from error that leads to death.

All teaching should be based squarely on God's word. We are competent to teach only as we are grounded in God's word ourselves. WE need to spend much time reading, studying, and memorizing the Word so that all we teach will conform to the Word of God.

- *I myself am convinced, my brothers, that you yourselves are full of goodness, complete in knowledge and competent to instruct one another.* Romans 15:14

- *All Scripture is God-breathed and is useful for teaching, rebuking, correcting and training in righteousness.* 2 Timothy 3:16

- *In everything set them an example by doing what is good. In your teaching show integrity, seriousness...* Titus 2:7

God intends for us to use our mouths to teach one another. Whether you are a preacher, a school teacher, a Sunday school teacher, a homeschool teacher, a mommy or daddy, a grandparent, an uncle, an aunt, a mentor, a friend, an older sibling, or a stranger on the street, whoever you are, you who are made in His image, should use your mouth to teach. Teaching about God and the gospel gives life. Teach about this most important thing in all eternity and give Him glory in the use of your mouth. But teaching about any simple wholesome subject: how to fry an egg, human philosophy, music composition, mathematics, the art of making friends, pottery, how to tie a shoe, how to paint a portrait, the care and feeding of sheep, entomology, poetry, horticulture, history, mud pie making or wildflower arranging, any subject taught to any person, if taught in the context of the gospel and in a manner true to reality is in some real sense life giving and life enhancing.

Some have a special gift and call as teachers in the church, but every believer's mouth should be used to teach. Be happy teaching. You are giving life!

Jesus' Mouth, the Image of God's Invisible Mouth

So much of what Jesus did with His mouth was to teach. A large portion of the gospels are taken up with the teachings of Jesus.

Jesus is our Rabbi, our teacher. This was the word that the multitudes used to address Him. His disciples frequently referred to Him as Rabbi. Of the ninety-some times Jesus was directly addressed in the gospels, sixty times He was called "Teacher". When Nicodemus came to Jesus by night he said, "We know that you are a teacher who has come from God. " (John 3:2)

Jesus used the term for Himself: "You call me Teacher and Lord, and rightly so, for that is what I am" (John 13:13)

He was the greatest teacher the world has ever known, even those who do not know Him as Savior and do not understand what He came to do for them think of Him as a great teacher.

Those interested in the field of pedagogy could do no better than to study Jesus' methods. Jesus used rhetorical tools such as proverbs, riddles, aphorisms, allegories, parables, and illustrations. He used visual aids and graphics. Jesus outshines even Socrates, the ostensible master of the effective use of questioning in teaching.

Jesus always wisely taught in a manner specific to His student. He addressed Himself personally to the person He was teaching. He knew them. He started where their heart was. He understood them and most important He loved them. Although it may not be taught to college education majors, love for the student is the most critical factor in successful teaching. All one has to do to recognize this truth is to think back over their own school experiences.

Jesus taught with an authority that astounded His listeners. If we are versed in the Word and base our teaching squarely upon His Word and on what Christ Himself accomplished on the cross, we too can teach with authority.

Jesus had a purpose and mission in all He taught. Everything He taught was part of His grand purpose of pointing His hearers to His Father, that they might know Him and His love.

If we desire mouths like His, no matter who we are or what our calling is, no matter how humble our education, or how young or old we are, or how shy we are, we will find ourselves speaking words that teach. Teaching is part of what our mouths were made for. Our Rabbi Jesus is the image of the invisible God who made our mouths in His image.

Lesson 20
Review Questions

What is the best preparation for being a life giving effective teacher?

Who can teach?

What does the word Rabbi mean?

MEMORIZE:

The teaching of the wise is a fountain of life, turning a man from the snares of death.
Proverbs 13:14

Lesson Twenty-One

Let Healing Words Fall like Rain

*Reckless words pierce like a sword, but **the tongue of the wise brings healing.***
Proverbs 12:18

The Mouth of The King's Child is the Mouth of a Healer.

J. R. R. Tolkien's Aragorn is a Christ-like character in a number of ways. One of the similarities is his healing hands. The ancient saying that "The hands of the king are the hands of a healer" is one means by which Aragorn's identity as true king was gradually revealed. The quietness, love, and simple beauty in that healing cannot help but remind Christian readers of Tolkien of the loving healing hands of our KING whose kingship was also recognized, at least by some, by his healing hands.

In the same manner it could be said of us, that, "The mouth of the KING'S child, is the mouth of a healer." We, like Jesus, who used both hands and mouth to bring healing, can (or should) be characterized as healers. Our mouths, like His, should be a great source of life-giving, life-sustaining healing. Our healing mouths should be one key to our identity as followers of Christ.

Words Can Heal

The Scriptures leave us with no doubt that words can heal. Words can be used to bring healing to physical, emotional, and spiritual ailments.

- *The **tongue that brings healing is a tree of life,** but a deceitful tongue crushes the spirit.* Proverbs 15:4

- *Pleasant words are a honeycomb, sweet to the soul and **healing to the bones.*** Proverbs 16:24

Words Heal Relationships

Part of our calling as healers is to be relationship healers, or peacemakers.

- *Reckless words pierce like a sword, but **the tongue of the wise brings healing.*** Proverbs 12:18

- *Blessed are the peacemakers, for they will be called sons of God.* Matthew 5:9

- *Let us therefore make every effort to do what leads to peace and to mutual edification.* Romans 14:19

111

- *Make every effort to keep the unity of the Spirit through the bond of peace.*
  Ephesians 4:3

Jesus' Mouth, the Image of God's Invisible Mouth

The healing mouth (and hands) of Christ are everywhere throughout the four gospels. You read about his healing in general terms as in these verses below as well as in many detailed personal stories.

- *Jesus went throughout Galilee, teaching in their synagogues, preaching the good news of the kingdom, and healing every disease and sickness among the people.*
  Matthew 4:23

- *Jesus went through all the towns and villages, teaching in their synagogues, preaching the good news of the kingdom and healing every disease and sickness.*
  Matthew 9:35

- *So they set out and went from village to village, preaching the gospel and healing people everywhere.* Luke 9:6

- *But the crowds learned about it and followed him. He welcomed them and spoke to them about the kingdom of God, and healed those who needed healing.* Luke 9:11

Jesus Words Brought Spiritual Healing

Malachi 2:6 appears to be a prophetic verse about the mouth of Christ, a flawless mouth that was used to turn many away from sin and bring spiritual healing.

True instruction was in his mouth and nothing false was found on his lips. He walked with me in peace and uprightness, and turned many from sin. Malachi 2:6

This beautiful verse helps us picture Christ, and it serves as a wonderful goal verse for our own mouths.

May God grant us mouths like Jesus' mouth, mouths that bring healing, so that together with Christ we will be a part of making "the sun of righteous rise with healing in its wings!"

Lesson 21
Review Questions

1. Maybe this discussion about "healing words" and being known as healers sounds lofty and unreal. Maybe it seems to belong more to idealized fantasy than everyday life. Maybe you have no idea what "healing words" would be. Try something.

   Can you remember any time in your own life when you were hurting; physically, emotionally, or spiritually, wounded by someone or some life experience and someone said something to you that helped a lot? Something that made you grow, or helped you recover from your pain? Those words were healing words.

   If you can recall any, write the words down, or at least the incident.

2. Write a brief theoretical scenario that would illustrate Proverbs 12:18 in action. *Reckless words pierce like a sword, but **the tongue of the wise brings healing.***

3. Is there anyone among your friends or family right now that is in need of some kind of healing? Can you think of any words, sound and true, based on God's word, that might bring healing?

MEMORIZE:

*Reckless words pierce like a sword, but **the tongue of the wise brings healing.***
Proverbs 12:18

*Pleasant words are a honeycomb, sweet to the soul and **healing to the bones.***
Proverbs 16:24

Part III: A Fountain of Life
Lesson Twenty-Two

Let Encouragement Flow

And let us consider how we may spur one another on towards love and good deeds. Let us not give up meeting together, as some are in the habit of doing, but let us encourage one another--and all the more as you see the Day approaching. Hebrews 10:24-25

If we want to have mouths that are fountains of life, like His, we need to cultivate the habit of encouraging because God is an awesome encourager. We have a great example to follow in Him.

- *May the God who <u>gives endurance and encouragement</u> give you a spirit of unity among yourselves as you follow Christ Jesus.* Romans 15:5

- *You hear, O LORD, the desire of the afflicted; <u>you encourage them</u>, and you listen to their cry.* Psalm 10:17

- <u>*For everything that was written in the past was written to teach us, so that through endurance and the encouragement of the Scriptures we might have hope.*</u> Romans 15:4

We also have the example of believers in the New Testament encouraging one another.

- *We sent Timothy, who is our brother and God's fellow worker in spreading the gospel of Christ, to strengthen and encourage you in your faith.* 1 Thessalonians 3:2

- *Judas and Silas, who themselves were prophets, said much to encourage and strengthen the brothers.* Acts 15:32

We are commanded to use our mouths for encouragement as well:

- *Therefore encourage one another and build each other up, just as in fact you are doing.* 1 Thessalonians 5:11

- *Therefore encourage each other with these words.* 1 Thessalonians 4:18

- *Let us not give up meeting together, as some are in the habit of doing, but let us encourage one another—and all the more as you see the Day approaching.* Hebrews 10:25

As is evident in both Hebrews 10:24-25 and 1 Thessalonians 2: 10 -12, encouragement means choosing careful words that will influence those who hear us to grow in godliness in some way. Encouragement spurs people on to love more deeply and more wisely and to grow in their understanding of how God wants us to live.

… Encouraging, comforting, and urging you to live lives worthy of God, who calls you into his kingdom and glory. 1 Thessalonians 2:12

And let us consider how we may spur one another on towards love and good deeds. Let us not give up meeting together, as some are in the habit of doing, but let us encourage one another--and all the more as you see the Day approaching. Hebrews 10:24-25

Two Simple Points about Being Effective Encouragers:

1. The only way encouragement can be truly effective is to base it solidly on God's word. To be good encouragers we need to be soaked in the scriptures so that they are our natural readily available source of wisdom.

    He must hold firmly to the trustworthy message as it has been taught, so that he can encourage others by sound doctrine and refute those who oppose it. Titus 1:9

2. The other condition of effective encouragement is "consider, consider, consider."

    The Hebrews ten passage above mentions "consideration" as a prerequisite to encouraging. We cannot effectively encourage someone if we have not taken the time and energy to consider their specific life, circumstances, experiences, their current situation, or their desires and needs. An effective encourager mulls over and meditates others' stories and understands them before they offer encouragement.

It is helpful to think of ourselves as on a long thorny journey together with all believers in a Pilgrim's Progress sort of way. We will all need encouragement in our turn as we encounter various troubles along the way. One day you will encourage me and another day I will need to encourage you. You may trip. I may stub my toe or lose my back pack. Someone else may wonder off the trail. We need to be there for each other. Our mouths can be a fountain of life to each other along this challenging path. Encouraging is something else God gave us mouths to do.

May our mouths be fountains of life as we encourage each other along the way.

Jesus' Mouth, the Image of God's Invisible Mouth

Jesus mouth flowed with encouragement to everyone in need.

His words in Mark 5:34 are typical of His encouragement. He said to her, "Daughter, your faith has healed you. Go in peace and be freed from your suffering."

But to see Jesus' mouth in action as an encourager most profoundly, read through chapters 14 through 17 of the book of John with a marker in hand. Imagine yourself as one of the disciples. Take a highlighter or marker and underline all the sentences and phrases where Christ is pouring forth encouragement. It flows from His mouth like a fountain and John seems to have tucked it all away in his heart.

"As the Father has loved me, so have I loved you. Now remain in my love. If you keep my commands, you will remain in my love, just as I have kept my Father's commands and remain in his love. I have told you this so that my joy may be in you and that your joy may be complete." John 15: 9-11

"Now is your time of grief, but I will see you again and you will rejoice, and no one will take away your joy." John 16:22

"I have told you these things, so that in me you may have peace. In this world you will have trouble. But take heart! I have overcome the world." John 16:33

May our mouths be fountains of life, as His was, as we encourage each other along the way.

Lesson 22
Review Questions

Define the word encouragement according to Hebrews 10:24-25 and 1 Thessalonians 2:10 -12.

What are two conditions of effective encouragement?

Think of someone who could use some encouraging. Mull over their life story. Consider their current situation and pray for wisdom to be an effective encourager for them.

MEMORIZE:

Therefore encourage one another and build each other up…

1 Thessalonians 5:11

Lesson Twenty-Three

Ahhh, Words of Comfort

Comfort, comfort my people, says your God. Isaiah 40:1

In this fallen world, we all need to be comforted. It's a universal need.

Poor Job. He needed comfort. He tells his miserable comforters what he would do if he were in their shoes.

> *But my mouth would encourage you; comfort from my lips would bring you relief.* Job 16:5

What a terrible job we often do at comforting, like Job's comforters, we give long-winded speeches to make ourselves feel good or important, but do not really address the pain or meet the need of those hurting, or even just stand with them experiencing their pain.

> *I have heard many things like these; miserable comforters are you all!* Job 16:2

And we all **are** miserable comforters. We even abandoned Jesus in his hour of great need. In Gethsemane he told his disciples, "My soul is overwhelmed with sorrow to the point of death." And we fell asleep.

Jesus needed comfort and found none because our sinful mouths are not used for the things they should be! Psalm 69, a Psalm about Christ, is heartbreaking. Careful reading of it should make us weep.

> *Scorn has broken my heart and has left me helpless; I looked for sympathy, but there was none, for comforters, but I found none.* Psalms 69:20

God incarnate did not receive the comfort he needed from us, but God is always ready with comfort for us.

- *As a mother comforts her child, so will I comfort you; and you will be comforted over Jerusalem."* Isaiah 66:13

- *But God, who comforts the downcast, comforted us ...* 2 Corinthians 7:6

Comforting comes natural to our heavenly father. God even comforts the angels!

> *So the LORD spoke kind and comforting words to the angel who talked with me.* Zechariah 1:13

Praise be to the God and Father of our Lord Jesus Christ, the Father of compassion and the God of all comfort, who comforts us in all our troubles, so that we can comfort those in any trouble with the comfort we ourselves have received from God. 2 Corinthians 1:3-4

We need to study how God uses His mouth, and use ours the same way! Part of His reason for comforting us is that we will learn to comfort one another.

God pleads with us to use our mouths to comfort each other!

Comfort, comfort my people, says your God. Isaiah 40:1

Jesus' Mouth, the Image of God's Invisible Mouth

Jesus, the very one we refused to comfort in His great time of need, at that same moment of great need in His own life, did not fail to offer profound comfort to those around Him.

He said to his disciples whose tongues offered Him no comfort in that Garden of Gethsemane, "Peace I leave with you; my peace I give you. I do not give to you as the world gives. Do not let your hearts be troubled and do not be afraid." John 14:27

Jesus mouth, our picture of the mouth of God, was generous with words of comfort to all who needed them. He speaks to us all: "Come unto me, all you who labor and are heavy laden, and I will give you rest." Matthew 11:28

Our mouths, which he died to redeem, are being remade in His image and part of that remaking will mean that we comfort one another as He comforted us.

Lesson 23
Review Questions

1. What are two of the most pointed instances of failure to provide comfort in the Bible?

2. God comforts us because he loves us and cares about us and pities us as a mother or father pities their children. But he also comforts us for another reason. What is that?

3. Is there an instance in your own life where you really needed comfort and did not get it? Is there an instance when you were blessed by a comforter? Can you think of an instance in which you failed to comfort when you should have?

MEMORIZE:

Comfort, comfort my people, says your God. Isaiah 40:1

Praise be to the God and Father of our Lord Jesus Christ, the Father of compassion and the God of all comfort, who comforts us in all our troubles, so that we can comfort those in any trouble with the comfort we ourselves have received from God. 2 Corinthians 1:3-4

Lesson Twenty-Four

Spout Wise Counsel

God is certainly the most suitable counselor! Who else could tell us what we need to hear as well as Him?

> *I will instruct you and teach you in the way you should go; I will counsel you and watch over you.* Psalm 32:8

> *All this also comes from the LORD Almighty, wonderful in counsel and magnificent in wisdom.* Isaiah 28:29

> *I will praise the LORD, who counsels me; even at night my heart instructs me.* Psalm 16:7

> *Counsel and sound judgment are mine; I have understanding and power.* Proverbs 8:14

> *Have I not written thirty sayings for you, sayings of counsel and knowledge?* Proverbs 22:20

We seek to reflect His mouth and use ours the way we are called to. We are told to use our mouths to give wise counsel based on God's words. We of course make pathetic counselors compared to an Almighty, all knowing Creator God. But we have at our disposal His words and His counsel for reference, and to the extent that our counsel to one another is squarely based on His Word to us, we also are competent to use our mouths for counsel.

- *Perfume and incense bring joy to the heart, and the pleasantness of one's friend springs from his earnest counsel.* Proverbs 27:9

- *For lack of guidance a nation falls, but many advisers make victory sure.* Proverbs 11:14

- *The mouth of the righteous man utters wisdom, and his tongue speaks what is just.* Psalm 37:30

- *I myself am satisfied about you, my brothers, that you yourselves are full of goodness, filled with all knowledge and able to instruct one another.* Romans 15:14

The secret for us in counseling is to know His word before we speak our words.

Jesus' Mouth, the Image of God's Invisible Mouth

This famous prophetic statement in the book of Isaiah about the coming Messiah presents us with a picture of the mouth of Jesus, the Wonderful Counselor.

For to us a child is born, to us a son is given, and the government will be on his shoulders. And he will be called Wonderful Counselor, Mighty God, Everlasting Father, Prince of Peace. Isaiah 9:6

Being renewed in the image of our Creator we now aim to be wonderful counselors in our own small way. May we too have the words to say to someone as lonely as Zacchaeus, words that can turn them around in one afternoon of counsel into a repentant and happy person -words like His.

Lesson 24
Review Questions

1. Who is THE WONDERFUL COUNSELOR?

2. How do we sit under the counsel of God?

3. On what basis are we competent to counsel?

4. What keeps you from offering counsel to others? What should you do about it?

MEMORIZE:

The mouth of the righteous man utters wisdom, and his tongue speaks what is just.
Psalm 37:30

Lesson Twenty-Five

Trickle Humble Exhortation and Loving Rebuke

One way to make our mouths a fountain of life like God's is to use them to exhort and to rebuke one another.

God brings life to us by never letting us go off in directions that lead to misery and death. He exhorts us and rebukes us to keep us going the right way. He does this because he loves us.

To a limited extent we can do this for one another too, and it is a wonderful life giving thing to do. We need this from each other. But it is thorny too. We are not all wise like God, and we often forget that about ourselves. We are not motivated by pure love like He is, though we often pretend to be. These facts make rebuking or exhorting very tricky and problematic.

God uses His mouth to lovingly rebuke us. All of God's words are useful for rebuking. They are good for correcting us! We are blessed to receive His rebukes. Meditate on the following verses and think about how blessed we are to have a loving God that cares enough to continue to exhort us and rebuke us.

- *All Scripture is God-breathed and is useful for teaching, rebuking, correcting and training in righteousness.* 2 Timothy 3:16

- *For these commands are a lamp, this teaching is a light, and the corrections of discipline are the way to life.* Proverbs 6:23

- *You rebuke and discipline men for their sin; you consume their wealth like a moth--each man is but a breath. Selah.* Psalms 39:11

- *You rebuke the arrogant, who are cursed and who stray from your commands.* Psalms 119:21

- *These things you have done and I kept silent; you thought I was altogether like you. But I will rebuke you and accuse you to your face.* Psalms 50:21

- *My son, do not despise the LORD's discipline and do not resent his rebuke.* Proverbs 3:11

God's rebuke is given in love and intended to bless!

- *If you had responded to my rebuke, I would have poured out my heart to you and made my thoughts known to you.* Proverbs 1:23

- *Those whom I love I rebuke and discipline. So be earnest, and repent.* Revelation 3:19

God calls us to rebuke and exhort each other.

- *Preach the Word; be prepared in season and out of season; correct, rebuke and encourage--with great patience and careful instruction.* 2 Timothy 4:2

He tells us that part of loving each other is to care enough to risk doing this very difficult thing with our mouths.

Do not hate your brother in your heart. Rebuke your neighbor frankly so that you will not share in his guilt. Leviticus 19:17

But knowing that we are limited, not all knowing, not wise, not without sin ourselves, God cautions us to rebuke with discretion.

- *Do not rebuke a mocker or he will hate you; rebuke a wise man and he will love you.* Proverbs 9:8

And to rebuke with humility and gentleness.

- *Do not rebuke an older man harshly, but exhort him as if he were your father. Treat younger men as brothers.* 1 Timothy 5:1

- *Those who oppose him he must gently instruct, in the hope that God will grant them repentance leading them to knowledge of the truth.* 2 Timothy 2:25

Although God does severely rebuke us, for our own good
 Out of His great love for us,
He cannot be characterized a God of exhortation and rebuke.
He is a God of love.
The driving force is His loving plan of redeeming His lost children.
At great cost and sacrifice He gives and gives.
Along with his wise and careful rebukes, God generously comforts, counsels, and encourages his children.
If God, who is perfectly righteous and perfectly within His rights to rebuke us anytime does not do it all the time; how much less should any of us be characterized as a REBUKER or an EXHORTOR! Exhort as prayerfully called for, but keep it rare.

Jesus' Mouth, the Image of God's Invisible Mouth

Christ exhorted all manner of us. He used strong language in His exhortation of the Sadducees and the Pharisees, the priests and the rulers. He exhorted the crowds and multitudes pointing out many ways in which their words and deeds were far from the path of their heavenly Father. He also earnestly exhorted His own beloved disciples sometimes using very strong words that stung. But every exhortation was conceived in love and had as its goal to point someone to the Father.

Christians need each other's help. We need accountability. We need to be willing to step into each other's messy lives and speak a loving word. None of us like the risk this involves. We often do not love enough to exhort each other. Study the gospels and make notes on Jesus' exhortations. Note who He exhorted, why, how, in what words, and if it is included in the narrative, what the results of His exhortation were. Ask God for the grace, wisdom, and love to exhort in the same way that He did. But we must always remember who He was and who we are. We need to take great care to remember our own frailty and faults when confronting others. We are not perfectly informed. We are not all wise. We are never pure in our motives. We are never without our own sin. May God make our mouths fruitful in this very delicate difficult calling of our mouths, exhortation. May our exhortations bring forth life!

Lesson 25
Review Questions

Define exhortation.

Define rebuke.

Why does it work so well for God to exhort and rebuke?

What big caution do we need to remember in letting rebuke or exhortation come from our mouths?

Why is it important not to just opt out of exhorting and rebuking since it is so delicate and tricky to do right?

MEMORIZE:

Do not hate your brother in your heart. Rebuke your neighbor frankly so that you will not share in his guilt.
Leviticus 19:17

Lesson Twenty-Six

Let Laughter Spill Over

God makes us happy. Just knowing Him, catching a glimpse of who He is and what He is like fills us with pleasure. God's abundant goodness delights and makes us overflow in laughter and songs of praise and joy.

- *There, in the presence of the LORD your God, you and your families shall eat and shall rejoice in everything you have put your hand to, because the LORD your God has blessed you.* Deuteronomy 12:7

- *And you and the Levites and the aliens among you shall rejoice in all the good things the LORD your God has given to you and your household.* Deuteronomy 26:11

- *Let the heavens rejoice, let the earth be glad; let the sea resound, and all that is in it.* Psalms 96:11

- *This is the day the LORD has made; let us rejoice and be glad in it.* Psalms 118:24

Having laughter come from our mouths, an overflow of joy in who God is and what he has done for us, is a mark of being a believer. It is a sign that we know the true God. He has moved us to laugh.

- *Our mouths were filled with laughter, our tongues with songs of joy. Then it was said among the nations, "The LORD has done great things for them."* Psalms 126:2

   God is the one who fills our mouths with laughter and as it spills over our mouths become fountains of life, pointing people to Him where they can find life.

- *He will yet fill your mouth with laughter and your lips with shouts of joy.* Job 8:21

Jesus' Mouth, the Image of God's Invisible Mouth

As we mentioned in Part Two of A MOUTH LIKE HIS, we know very little for certain about Jesus and laughter. The Bible nowhere mentions that he laughed, but it certainly does not rule out His having laughed. I think in fact most of us familiar with who He is would agree that it is almost certain that He smiled often and that He did laugh, despite the seriousness of His purpose and the heaviness of His calling. He was a man of sorrows and acquainted with grief, but He was also a person of the Trinity acquainted with all the joy and wonder of His creation and familiar with its delights. We know that God the

Father, Son, and Holy Spirit enjoyed creating the world and human kind and delighted in the work of it together. Proverbs eight paints a picture of the Godhead almost frolicking for joy in their task of creation.

"Then I was constantly at his side. I was filled with delight day after day, rejoicing always in his presence rejoicing in his whole world and delighting in mankind." Proverbs 8:30-31

Jesus also would have responded in deep joy to the work of His Father and rejoiced as the Old Testament verses quoted above commanded God's people to do.

Jesus was so loving and we so child-like to Him that He must also have smiled at His disciples sometimes and perhaps even broken out into hearty laughter over our small limited point of view, as a loving parent might laugh when they discover their toddler's touching funny perception of something to be delightful.

Although in this instance we have less to go on in observation of Christ's earthly example, there is no doubt that the laughter of Jesus will ring out across eternity when all His work is brought to fruition at the end of time as we know it. For it is He that will fill our mouths with laughter and His mighty work on our behalf that will fill our lips with shouts of joy! (Job 8:21)

Lesson 26
Review Questions

What is the deepest reason for real laughter? (The kind of laughter that is more than a response to a silly joke.)

This lesson is about laughter as a fountain of life. Does the fact that laughter is a fountain of life infer that entertaining is too? Wholesome entertaining? In our entertainment saturated culture this is something worth thinking about. You might want to review the end of lesson 12.

There are many different opinions about whether Jesus had a sense of humor. Did he try to evoke laughs via entertaining words? The expression of various positions make fascinating reading. The question makes an interesting discussion. Despite the fact that we know so little and so much is conjecture, contemplating Christ's example in any area, even in areas where we have little to go by, when we look carefully at what we do know, can unearth helpful thoughts. Prepare for a discussion about this subject. What do you think about it? What do you base your thoughts on?

At what point in history do we know that Jesus delighted and rejoiced?

In what way is laughter like a fountain of life?

MEMORIZE:

Our mouths were filled with laughter, our tongues with songs of joy. Then it was said among the nations, "The LORD has done great things for them."
Psalm 126:2

Lesson Twenty-Seven

Spurt Out the Good News!

TESTIFY

One thing God certainly made our mouths for is that we might testify. To testify is to stand up for something and be willing to confirm that it is so. You saw it, or heard it, or you know it to be true and if the truth about what you know is in question, you speak out to let people know what you saw or heard. This is a testimony.

A testimony can be about simple things.

"I know where your book is, I saw it fall behind the couch."

Or about more important things:

"The man in the black sweater is the one who took the old lady's pocket book. I saw him take it. He dropped it behind that bush over there. "

Or about THE very MOST important thing:

"I know that Christ is alive. He has done great things for me. I was a different person before. I used to be full of anger and despair, but now I have hope and joy. When Christ came into my life, he made me a new person. I have a happy life and a good family now. God is so good. "

These are all testimonies. Our mouths were made for giving right and true testimonies at the right moments.

God made laws about testimonies and people and government make laws about them too.

- *One witness is not enough to convict a man accused of any crime or offence he may have committed. A matter must be established by the testimony of two or three witnesses.* Deuteronomy 19:15

An honest, completely true testimony is very important to God. One of His top ten laws, the ten commandments, is about giving honest testimony.

You shall not give false testimony against your neighbor. Exodus 20:16

THE ULTIMATE TESTIMONY

The most significant testimony anyone can give is this one:

- *And this is the testimony: God has given us eternal life, and this life is in his Son.* 1 John 5:11

The Samaritan woman at the well made her mouth a fountain of life, because she gave testimony and that testimony lead to LIFE for many!

- *Many of the Samaritans from that town believed in him because of the woman's testimony, "He told me everything I ever did.* John 4:39

We should be like the Samaritan woman at the well. The New Testament gives us several examples of people striving to be fountains of life by sharing the good news of the gospel of Christ.

Paul asks people to pray that his mouth would be a fountain of life in this way.

- *Pray also for me, that whenever I open my mouth, words may be given me so that I will fearlessly make known the mystery of the gospel.* Ephesians 6:19

How can they hear if no one tells them?

The most direct and important way in which our mouths are meant to be Fountains of Life, is to **make life possible** for many who would otherwise die. By sharing the good news of Christ's love and sacrificial death we bring life. This is our privilege, our calling, our joy.

- *How, then, can they call on the one they have not believed in? And how can they believe in the one of whom they have not heard? And how can they hear without someone preaching to them?* Romans 10:14

- *That which was from the beginning, which we have heard, which we have seen with our eyes, which we have looked at and our hands have touched--this we proclaim concerning the Word of life. The life appeared; we have seen it and testify to it, and we proclaim to you the eternal life, which was with the Father and has appeared to us.* 1 John 1:1-2

Jesus' Mouth, the Image of God's Invisible Mouth

Jesus used His mouth to testify about who He was and what God had sent Him to do.

For God so loved the world that he gave his one and only Son, that whoever believes in him shall not perish but have eternal life. For God did not send his Son into the world to condemn the world, but to save the world through him. Whoever believes in him is not condemned, but whoever does not believe stands condemned already because they have not believed in the name of God's one and only Son. This is the verdict: Light has come into the world, but people loved darkness instead of light because their deeds were evil. Everyone who does evil hates the light, and will not come into the light for fear that their deeds will be exposed. But whoever lives by the truth comes into the light, so that it may be seen plainly that what they have done has been done in the sight of God. John 3:16 - 21

The Father loves the Son and has placed everything in his hands. Whoever believes in the Son has eternal life, but whoever rejects the Son will not see life, for God's wrath remains on them. John 3: 35-36

Jesus set an example of giving testimony about God's loving plan that brought life to people. He also made sure we knew what to do with our mouths before he returned to heaven. He gave us a special job.

THE GREAT COMMISION = A JOB FOR OUR MOUTHS

- *Then Jesus came to them and said, "All authority in heaven and on earth has been given to me. Therefore go and make disciples of all nations, baptising them in the name of the Father and of the Son and of the Holy Spirit, and teaching them to obey everything I have commanded you. And surely I am with you always, to the very end of the age.* Matthew 28:18-20

- *But you will receive power when the Holy Spirit comes on you; and you will be my witnesses in Jerusalem, and in all Judea and Samaria, and to the ends of the earth.* Acts 1:8

Sharing the gospel and thereby bringing life through Christ to those without hope is the most beautiful way to make our mouths a fountain of life.

Lesson 27
Review Questions

Jesus tells us to be his witnesses. What tool is essential for a witness?

Explain how the Samaritan woman's mouth was a fountain of life.

Have you ever shared the gospel with anyone? Can you articulate the gospel? Describe the good news of the gospel in a few sentences as though you were telling a friend you just met what you believe is true.

MEMORIZE:

Pray also for me, that whenever I open my mouth, words may be given me so that I will fearlessly make known the mystery of the gospel.
Ephesians 6:19

Lesson Twenty-Eight

LET CONFESSION FLOW

Confession holds a very special place in scripture. Of all the important things our mouths were made to do, this is among the most important. The Bible speaks about confession of two things. Often the two go together. They are certainly related.

It speaks of confessing our sins and confessing our faith.

CONFESSION OF OUR SINS A CONFESSION TO GOD

We acknowledge that we have sinned and that it is awful and heinous in God's sight. We ask for forgiveness. This is confession of sin.

Then I acknowledged my sin to you and did not cover up my iniquity. I said, "I will confess my transgressions to the LORD" --and you forgave the guilt of my sin.
Psalms 32:5

Psalm 51 provides a beautiful and powerful example of David's prayer of confession.

Psalm 51

For the director of music. A psalm of David. When the prophet Nathan came to him after David had committed adultery with Bathsheba.

[1] Have mercy on me, O God,
   according to your unfailing love;
   according to your great compassion
   blot out my transgressions.

[2] Wash away all my iniquity
   and cleanse me from my sin.

[3] For I know my transgressions,
   and my sin is always before me.

[4] Against you, you only, have I sinned
   and done what is evil in your sight,
   so that you are proved right when you speak
   and justified when you judge.

[5] Surely I was sinful at birth,
   sinful from the time my mother conceived me.

[6] Surely you desire truth in the inner parts [a] ;
   you teach [b] me wisdom in the inmost place.

[7] Cleanse me with hyssop, and I will be clean;
   wash me, and I will be whiter than snow.

[8] Let me hear joy and gladness;
   let the bones you have crushed rejoice.

[9] Hide your face from my sins
   and blot out all my iniquity.

[10] Create in me a pure heart, O God,
   and renew a steadfast spirit within me.

[11] Do not cast me from your presence
   or take your Holy Spirit from me.

[12] Restore to me the joy of your salvation
   and grant me a willing spirit, to sustain me.

[13] Then I will teach transgressors your ways,
   and sinners will turn back to you.

[14] Save me from bloodguilt, O God,
   the God who saves me,
   and my tongue will sing of your righteousness.

[15] O Lord, open my lips,
   and my mouth will declare your praise.

We are blessed by the promise that when we confess our sins, God will forgive us! It is not a "might or might not." It is not according to his mood or whim. **If we confess, He will** forgive. A wonderful gift, a wonderful promise! We should take advantage of it!

> *If we confess our sins, he is faithful and just and will forgive us our sins and purify us from all unrighteousness.* 1 John 1:9

CONFESS TO ONE ANOTHER

We are also told that it is good to confess our sins to each other. Admit them. Seek forgiveness from each other and ask for help that we might not sin again.

> *Therefore confess your sins to each other and pray for each other so that you may be healed. The prayer of a righteous man is powerful and effective.* James 5:16

CONFESSION OF OUR FAITH

The other kind of confession, is confession of our faith.

We confess that we believe. God wants us to confess our faith in Christ. This of course also assumes the confession of our sins and the need for Christ's blood to cover them.

People who hear the gospel and believe it confess their faith and are baptized. They "become Christians." If you grow up in a Christian family, when you are old enough to understand the wonder and truth of the gospel for yourself and acknowledge that Christ is God and also perfect man, that he died to take on himself payment for your sins, when you comprehend how totally you need Jesus as your own Savior, we say you are "confessing Christ". Christian churches have different doctrines and practices regarding the children of believers confessing their faith. In baptistic churches a young person would be baptized at this time. In paedobaptist churches when a young person who was baptized as an infant of believing parents confesses their faith they begin to take the Lord's Supper. Challenging doctrinal distinctives aside, all Christians agree that confessing Christ as their only savior and Lord is critically important to our salvation and is Biblically mandated.

God made our mouths with a purpose of confessing His name! Look at Hebrews 13:15. The fruit, the purpose, or the result of our lips, is confession of His name.

There is to be a continual confession of His name! His name should be frequently on our lips! We should be always mentioning him and our faith in him.

> *Through Jesus, therefore, let us **continually** offer to God a sacrifice of praise-- the **fruit of lips that confess his name**.* Hebrews 13:15

A mouth that confesses Christ is a fountain of life.

Lesson 28
Review Questions

Read verses one through four of Psalm 51. We all know that David hurt Bathsheba, her husband, and many other people by this sin. Why does David say, " Against you, you only, have I sinned and done what is evil in your sight, so that you are proved right when you speak   and justified when you judge." ?

Do you make a practice of confessing your sins to other people? Can you think of a time when you have done this recently?

Why do we need to continue to confess Christ, having done so once?

MEMORIZE:

Then I acknowledged my sin to you and did not cover up my iniquity. I said, "I will confess my transgressions to the LORD" --and you forgave the guilt of my sin.
Psalms 32:5

PART IV

A FULL CIRCLE
AND
THE CLIMAX OF IT ALL

INTRODUCTION TO PART IV

A FULL CIRCLE AND THE CLIMAX OF IT ALL

In Part I of this study we considered what the mouth of God is like. Astounding! We realized it could be characterized as a "fountain of life." We discussed how we, as creatures made in his image, were intended to have mouths like his. In our sinful natures we utterly fail.

In Part II we looked at all the ways in which we sin with our mouths. No matter how noble our efforts to train the guard of our mouth, no matter how earnestly we want to fend off the types of words we discussed in the lessons in Part II, we fail. We stand accountable to God for our sinful mouths, for every careless word.

In PART III we looked at all the ways in which God does intend for us to use our mouths, the types of speech that would turn our mouths into fountains of life, like his. But here too, we fall hopelessly short. We are unable to live up to these high callings for our mouth.

The last two lessons in this course finally hold out hope! In this brief PART IV we pick up with the discussion of confession that concluded Part III. There are two more important ideas taught in Scripture about confession that amazingly pull together all we have considered and bring it to a poignant climax. God's Word is amazing and offers us amazing hope. Everything comes round in full circle. Hope appears. There is suddenly a way to live like we are made in his image. At last hope materializes for having a mouth like His!

Lesson Twenty-Nine

HOPE FOR HAVING A MOUTH LIKE HIS

We concluded Part III with the thought that confession is one way that our mouths can be a fountain of life. It is through believing in our hearts and confessing our faith in Christ with our mouths that we are saved!

*That if you confess with your mouth, "Jesus is Lord," and believe in your heart that God raised him from the dead, you will be saved. For it is with your heart that you believe and are justified, **and it is with your mouth that you confess and are saved.*** Romans 10:9-10

When we confess Christ as our Savior and LORD, we have life! Confession from our mouths brings about life -- NEW LIFE FOR US IN CHRIST, and this new life in Christ gives us a new heart.

Our mouths are to be a fountain of life. If we use them to confess our sins and to confess Christ, they are indeed a fountain of life, bringing forth life first of all for ourselves in Christ. We have a new heart. And here we find the amazing satisfying completion of all we have been studying in this course – a full complete circle.

This NEW HEART enables us to use our mouths in all the ways we have been discussing. We have seen that in our own strength, in our own old self, we cannot train the guard of our mouth to keep watch over the door of our mouths. David cried out to God to put a guard there for him. He knew he could not stop himself from saying all the things he should not say.

Neither can we make our mouths to be a fountain of life like God's mouth without a new heart. Apart from confessing Christ we are doomed. Our mouths are doomed. They will not obey us even if we KNOW what we are to do and not to do with them! Our mouth, like the rest of our body is dead in sin. Only in our confessing Christ, receiving new life and a new heart can our mouths also be redeemed and again be mouths working as they were meant to, mouths after the image of God's great, awesome, powerful life giving mouth!

The Bible says clearly that out of the heart, the mouth speaks.

- *You brood of vipers, how can you who are evil say anything good? For out of the overflow of the heart the mouth speaks.* Matthew 12:34

- *But the things that come out of the mouth come from the heart, and these make a man `unclean'.* Matthew 15:18

But when we come to Christ we are made new and have new hearts, there is then finally hope for our mouths to be like His mouth!

- *I will give you a new heart and put a new spirit in you; I will remove from you your heart of stone and give you a heart of flesh.* Ezekiel 36:26

There we have the perfect circle allowing us to hope for a mouth like His. With our mouth we confess Christ, confessing Him we receive a new heart, originating in this new heart, new words flow out from mouths that are now truly like His.

Christ on the cross freed us to be who we were made to be. He has enabled us to be renewed in knowledge in the image of our creator. A look at this history of our mouths has revealed God's loving plan to redeem us!

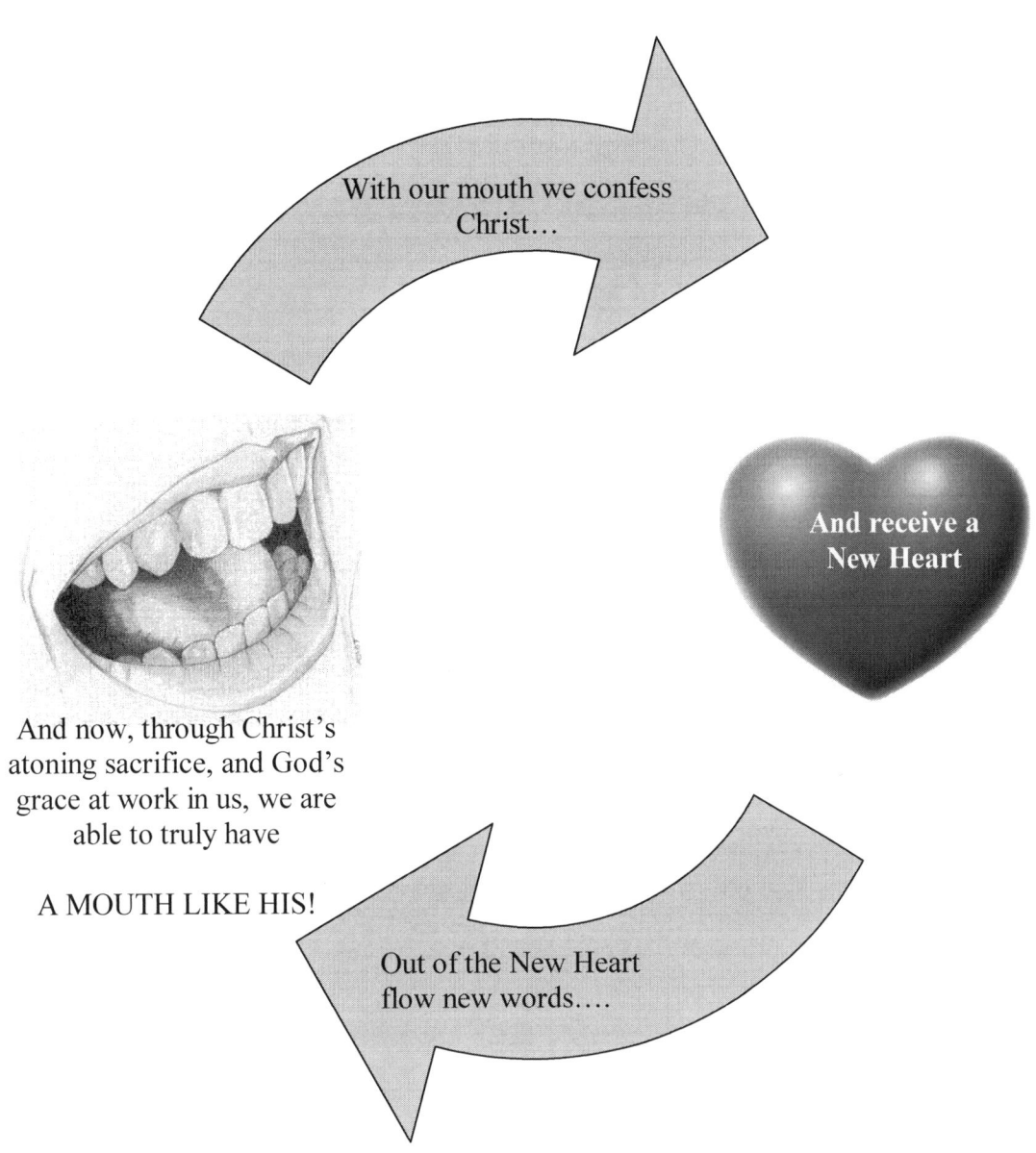

With our mouth we confess Christ...

And receive a New Heart

And now, through Christ's atoning sacrifice, and God's grace at work in us, we are able to truly have

A MOUTH LIKE HIS!

Out of the New Heart flow new words....

But the things that come out of the mouth come from the heart, and these make a man 'unclean'.
Matthew 15:18

I will give you a new heart and put a new spirit in you; I will remove from you your heart of stone and give you a heart of flesh.
Ezekiel 36:26

Lesson 29
Review Questions

Diagram the perfect circle that completes our hope for really having mouths like His. Write out Matthew 15:18 and Ezekiel 36:26 under it.

MEMORIZE:

But the things that come out of the mouth come from the heart, and these make a man `unclean'.
Matthew 15:18

and

I will give you a new heart and put a new spirit in you; I will remove from you your heart of stone and give you a heart of flesh.
Ezekiel 36:26

Lesson Thirty

THE CLIMAX OF THE HISTORY OF MOUTHS

The Bible tells us one more important thing about confessing mouths.

The final word about confessing is that there will come a day when God will make every tongue confess. Every tongue will do what it was made to do.

The ultimate purpose of every human mouth will be fulfilled.

Philippians chapter two describes a great climax for all the mouths of all history!

> *Therefore God exalted him to the highest place and gave him the name that is above every name, that at the name of Jesus every knee should bow, in heaven and on earth and under the earth, **and every tongue confess** that Jesus Christ is Lord, to the glory of God the Father.*

> Philippians 2:9-11

God will have every human tongue fulfill its true purpose. Every tongue, even those that for their life time denied the truth, and would not confess, will do so.

Every tongue, in every mouth, on every face; yellow, brown, black, red, and white, all the mouths that have ever been, mouths from every country, mouths from every culture, mouths from every period of human history, will one day do what they were ultimately created for! They will confess that Jesus Christ is LORD! They will remember that God created them. They will acknowledge that Jesus lived the way they should have lived, that he had a mouth like they should have had, and that God graciously offered them forgiveness through Christ's atoning death.

What an amazing moment that will be. Imagine it! The pinnacle of all history. And certainly the high point of the history of human mouths!

May we confess Him now, and not wait until that glorious and severe day when God moves our tongue for us to make it confess.

If we put our faith and trust in Christ's living and dying for us, now, and confess our faith with our mouths, now, we will be saved. We will have a new life, and a new heart. All the sins of our mouths will be forgiven. Our mouths will be reckoned as pure and beautiful as the mouth of Christ who guarded His perfectly and used it as a fountain of life. And by grace, life giving words will flow out from our new hearts, and our mouths will be like His!

Lesson 30
Review Questions

Imagine this great day, this climax of the history of all human mouths. Picture every mouth from all time, confessing that Jesus Christ is Lord!

Respond to this moving vision with a sketch, painting, poem, prose, or song. (yours or someone else's that suits this amazing moment in history.)

Use the blank page beside this one for your response. Then look at the two sample responses that follow.

MEMORIZE:

Therefore God exalted him to the highest place and gave him the name that is above every name, that at the name of Jesus every knee should bow, in heaven and on earth and under the earth, **and every tongue confess** *that Jesus Christ is Lord, to the glory of God the Father.*

Philippians 2:9-11

PART IV: The Circle and the Climax

"At the name of Jesus every knee should bow in heaven and on the earth and under the earth, and every tongue confess that Jesus Christ is Lord."
Philippians 2:10, 11

"And the glory of the LORD will be revealed and all mankind together will see it. For the MOUTH of the LORD has spoken."
Isaiah 40:5

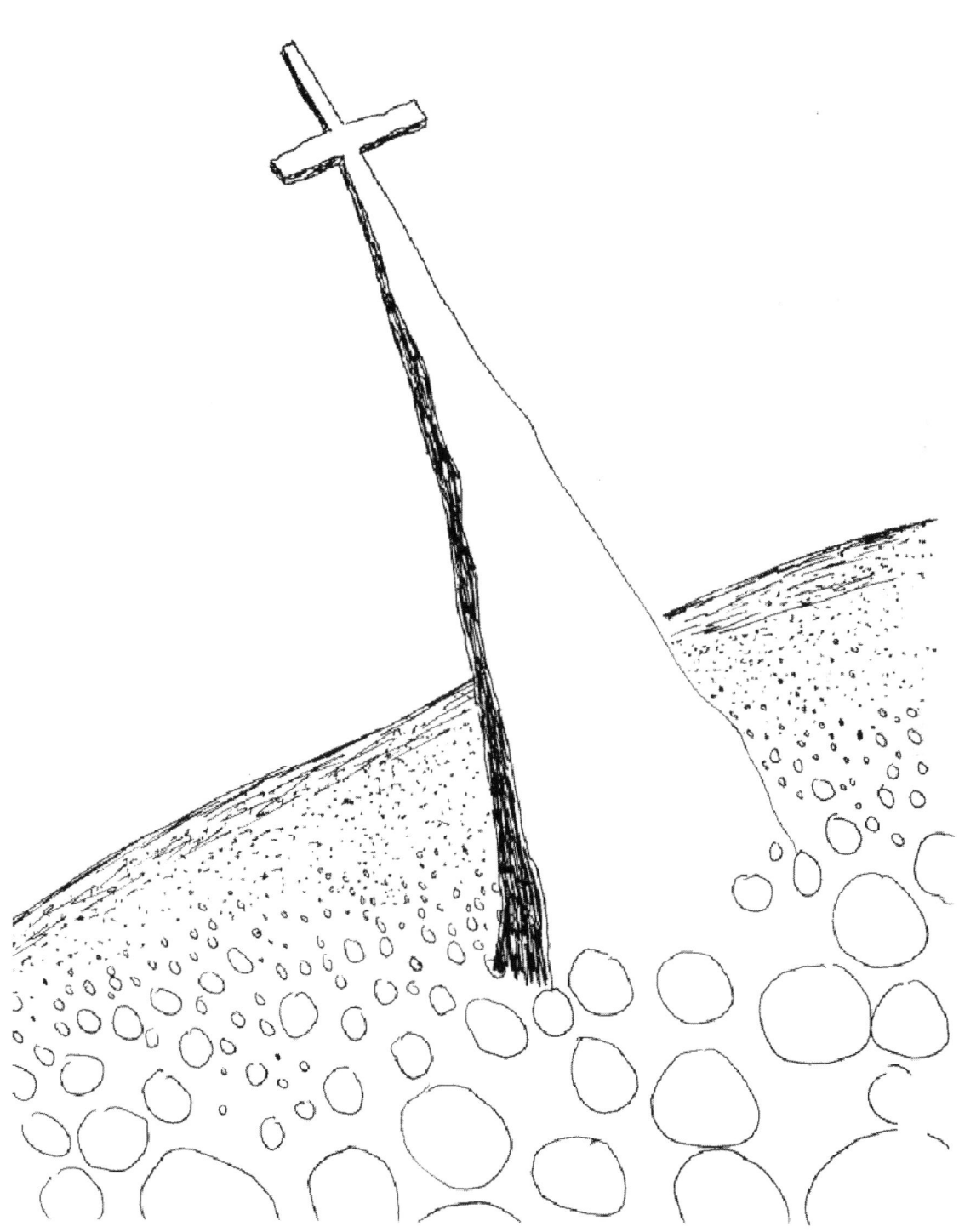

Springs of Living Water

Today we are in the middle of the story, but it is a story that we know the end of with certainty. We need to live in the present with the end in view.

Today we still struggle with temptation. We are tempted to lie, to use words recklessly, to gossip, to boast, to use angry words, to use divisive words, to curse, even to take our Lord's name in vain, to be obnoxious and loud, to be silly, to speak like a fool, to be critical and to let our mouths run with too many words. Today we are still in the process of training the guard of our mouths and we often need to cry out for God's help.

At this point in time we are only beginning to experience the marvelous life giving power of our tongues. We are feeble and pathetic in our efforts to repeat and practice our Father's words and learn His language. Our praise is scarce and pathetic. We do not give thanks as we should. We only rarely give godly instruction. Our mouths are only infrequently tools of healing. Encouragement only trickles, as do words of comfort. Our counsel is not as well grounded in His word as it should be, and our exhortations are sometimes harsh or unwise. We do not often share the glorious truth of the gospel and our confessions are reluctant and sparse.

Nevertheless, Christ laid down His life to redeem our mouths. Because of Him our words now flow out from a new heart and we can hold on to the reality that there is a tremendous power for good, a life giving power, in our mouths.

How delightful it will be when our mouths are one day perfectly like His, when God has completed the good work He has begun in us. Meanwhile we need to remember who we are in Christ and live rooted and built up in Him. We need to recall that we have been rescued from the dominion of darkness and brought into the kingdom of light where the guard of our mouths can see clearly what to keep from our lips. We need to recall that we *"have put on the new self, which is being renewed in knowledge in the image of its Creator."* Through Christ even now we can have mouths that are substantially like His mouth – a mouth that speaks words that bring forth life! Remember when Jesus told the woman at the well that if she drank of Him, springs of living water would flow out through her? That's who we are. Having come to the living waters and having drank of Christ, we have within us a spring welling up to eternal life ready to burst forth and be spread to all those around us. No wonder Proverbs calls the mouth of the righteous a fountain of life! That spring of water welling up to eternal life comes out and flows to others mostly through the words of our mouths.

By God's grace may we use our powerful mouths to bless others around us. May the words we speak bring life and hope and healing and joy. May those around us be refreshed by the words coming from our mouths. The righteousness of Christ is ours, and the mouths of the righteous are a fountain of life. Believe this about your mouth. Stand in awe of the beauty and potential of the mouth He has given you and redeemed for you – It's a mouth like His!

A CLOSING PRAYER

Father in Heaven, You who spoke all things into being:

I praise you for the mighty power of your words. Your words always accomplish what you will. Your words are utterly dependable and true. Your words gave me life. They sustain me.

Father, thank you for the incredible never ending love you have for me, throughout all ages you planned a means of bringing me home to you and making all things right after I had lost my way. Thank you for sending Jesus, your ultimate Word. He is the image of you that I needed in order to know you, and His sacrifice on the cross paid for all the sins of my fallen mouth.

Father, renew in me the knowledge of who you are. You created me in your image. Now, in Christ, redeem that likeness. Make my mouth a mouth like yours.

God, you promised those who come to you, that a spring of living water would well up in them and flow out. Let that spring flow out through my words to wash over and bring life and hope and joy and healing to all around me. Please, God, make my mouth a fountain of life like yours.

I ask through Christ, Your Ultimate Word
Amen

Appendix A
Theme Song Lyrics
His Mouth is a Fountain of Life

1

E   B
God said, "Let there be," and there was.
 F#m A E
Nothing is - that he did not speak
     A
How awesome is the mouth of God
 C#m
His words create
 B
His words sustain
 F#m A E
His mouth is a fountain of life.

CHORUS:
E
Every word flawless
F#m   A
Every word true
C#m B A
Every word utterly kind
    B E
Every one achieves His will.
E   A
Like a mirror, like bread, like fire
C#m   B A
His words are sufficient for me.
    B E
Grass withers. Flowers fall.
  C#m A B E
But His words stand firm forever.
 F#m A E
His mouth is a fountain of life.

2

My mouth in his image was made
A precious gift resembling his
And like my God I think and speak
My words like sparks
Produce a blaze
Death and life in my tongue's power

3

O Lord set a guard at my lips
Restrain unwholesome words.
Pray keep a tight rein on my tongue
Lies and folly
Anger, complaints
I'll give account for every word

4

I want my mouth like yours.
Yours is flawless. Mine so corrupt.
Wrong words are conceived in my heart
Make my heart new
Through Jesus Christ
New hearts bear words that bring forth life

5

May each word I speak build up
Every word accomplish your will
Let me tell others of Christ's death
Words bringing life
Let each word count
Make my mouth a fountain of life.

6

One day all mouths will submit
Every tongue will say, "He is Lord."
For those three words all mouths were made.
In Christ we'll rise
Voices fill the skies
Praising the fountain of life

Appendix B
Bible Memory Chart

Bible Memory Progress

		Bible Memory Verses	check
Lesson 1	God's Awesome Mouth: Characteristic 1	Psalm 33:6	
Lesson 2	God's Awesome Mouth: Character 2 - 6	Isaiah 55:11 & Isaiah 40:8	
Lesson 3	Mouths Like His – The Beautiful Ideal	James 3: 4-5 & Proverbs 18:21	
Lesson 4	Mouths Like His – The Sad Reality	Psalm 141:3 & Proverbs 30:5	
Lesson 5	Imprison Ugly Lies	Proverbs 12:22	
Lesson 6	Arrest Reckless Words	Proverbs 12:18	
Lesson 7	Confine Gossip	Proverbs 11:13	
Lesson 8	Incarcerate Boasting	Galatians 6:14	
Lesson 9	Detain Angry Words	James 1: 19- 20	
Lesson 10	Divisive Words & Any That Tear Down	Romans 12:18 & Ephesians 4:29	
Lesson 11	Catch Curses Protect the Lord's Name	Exodus 20:7	
Lesson 12	Jail Obnoxious, Disruptive, and Silly	Ephesians 5:4	
Lesson 13	Demolish Foolish Words	Proverbs 15:2	
Lesson 14	Capture Complaining and Grumbling	Philippians 2:14 -15	
Lesson 15	Take Critical Words into Custody	Proverbs 11:12	
Lesson 16	Confiscate Too-Many-Words	Proverbs 10:19	
Lesson 17	Floods of Repetition	Joshua 1:8	
Lesson 18	Gush With Praise	Psalm 71:8	
Lesson 19	Overflow with Thanksgiving	Psalm 95:2 & Romans 1:21	
Lesson 20	Spew out Godly Instruction	Proverbs 13:14	
Lesson 21	Let Healing Words Fall Like Rain	Proverbs 12:18 & 16:24	
Lesson 22	Let Encouragement Flow	1 Thessalonians 5:11	
Lesson 23	Ahhh, Words of Comfort	Isaiah 40:1 & 2 Corinthians 1:3-4	
Lesson 24	Spout Wise Counsel	Psalm 37:30	
Lesson 25	Trickle Exhortation and Rebuke	Leviticus 19:17	
Lesson 26	Let Laughter Spill Over	Psalm 126:2	
Lesson 27	Spurt out the Good News	Ephesians 6:19	
Lesson 28	Let Confession Flow	Psalm 32:5	
Lesson 29	Hope For Having a Mouth Like His	Matthew 15:18 & Ezekiel 36:26	
Lesson 30	The Climax of the History of Mouths	Philippians 2:9-11	

Appendix C
A Word on the Pedagogy

A Mouth Like His has been fruitfully used in a variety of contexts by a variety of ages.

It has been effectively used as:

- A personal devotional study for adults or teens

- Family Worship Material – It spans the ages in a large family well from elementary school ages through adults

- Sunday School (*A Mouth Like His* has been effectively used in an age integrated class, in middle school classes and as a high school class.)

- Home School Bible Course for a family or a co op.

- Christian School – A Mouth Like His makes a lively dramatic Bible class with a clear gospel presentation and solid life changing Biblical content.

Lessons are Enhanced and Retained through Bible Memory

This *Mouth Like His* study is greatly enhanced by the memorization of the Bible verses presented at the end of each lesson. Bible memory, as mentioned in lesson 17, is one way to learn the language of our Heavenly Father. Parents or teachers should encourage this memory work and recitation and keep track of it, and if possible should set an example by doing the memory work along with the students. A chart is provided in Appendix B in the back of each book to keep track of progress, and a file for printing flash cards is also available. See below.

Incorporate Drama and Visuals

In a Sunday school, Vacation Bible School, Christian school, or Homeschool Co-Op settings, performing lively skits to illustrate and practice the application of the lessons is both fun and helpful. It enhances the message of each lesson as well as making it stick in the students' memories.

The concept of positioning a guard over our lips in Part II of A Mouth Like His is easy to illustrate in a dramatic way. We constructed a large mouth out of a queen sized flat white bed sheet, painting a mouth on the fabric and cutting out the opening of the mouth large enough for students to move in and out through the mouth as though they are words. A piece of black fabric hangs behind the mouth with room to come and go. A Pocket is sewn along the top of the sheet and the sheet is hung on a long rod. A guard dressed in full armor with a sword in hand guards the lips in various skits written to reinforce the lessons.

For Part III of *A Mouth Like His* we made a giant poster of a fountain. Each drop of water has a piece of Velcro on it to attach a paper water droplet inscribed with one of the types of words that make our mouths into fountains of life: "Instruction", "confession", "praise", "thanksgiving", "comfort", "exhortation", etc. Each week we Velcro up another droplet as we study a new lesson, making the water fountain more and more full and beautiful as we go along.

Tools Available for Free

An MP₃ File of the theme song: *His Mouth is a Fountain of Life* is available for free downloading.

Theme Song Lyrics – A copy of the song lyrics is included in Appendix A in each book. Feel free to make as many copies of the lyrics as you wish.

Bible Memory Cards-
This study is most effective when the Bible memory work is done in conjunction with it. Files for the backs and fronts of Bible Memory Flash Cards are available (free) to download, print out on cardstock, and cut up.

Skits- In a Sunday school, Vacation Bible School, Christian school or Homeschool Co-Op setting performing lively skits to illustrate the lessons is both fun and helpful and enhances the message of each lesson as well as making it stick in the students' memories. Part II of *A Mouth Like His* is particularly fun to illustrate with a giant mouth and a guard standing at the lips. A number of sample skits written and used in the past are available for your perusal. You are welcome to print them out if you'd like to use them.

Photos of "The Mouth" – If you are interested in the idea of making a giant mouth and need some inspiration we are happy to share a photo of our giant "sheet mouth" to get you started.

To receive any of these free helps contact Faye Hake via email
fayehake@idothisbecause.org

22227075R00099

Made in the USA
Middletown, DE
23 July 2015